ORIENTAL
MYSTICS
&
MAGICIANS

ORIENTAL MYSTICS

&

MAGICIANS

PERLE EPSTEIN

DOUBLEDAY & COMPANY, INC., GARDEN CITY, NEW YORK

MY THANKS TO DONALD WEISER WITHOUT WHOSE
INVALUABLE ASSISTANCE THIS BOOK COULD NOT HAVE
BEEN WRITTEN.

Library of Congress Cataloging in Publication Data

Epstein, Perle S
Oriental mystics & magicians.

Bibliography: p. 153
1. East—Religion. 2. Magic—East. 3. Religions
—Biography. I. Title.
BL1035.E65   291.6′2
ISBN 0-385-02338-3 Trade
        0-385-08343-2 Prebound
Library of Congress Catalog Card Number 74–22407

FOR MIMI KRAMER

CONTENTS

PREFACE   9

INDIA   17

SRI CHAITANYA   35

JAPAN   43

THE ZEN MASTER HAKUIN   53

CHINA   63

TIBET   85

JETSUN MILAREPA   119

RAMAKRISHNA   133

BIBLIOGRAPHY   153

PREFACE

In the East, everything is possible. Or, to put it another way, everything is illusion. Opposite statements that, to the Zen-trained riddle-reader or yogi, make as much sense as "one plus one equal two" does to you and me. *Super*natural events, as such, don't exist for the person who believes that *all* events (whether *super* or *natural*) are mere projections springing from the mind of Brahma—the eternal Creative Force behind what we would consider "the world." From the Hindu point of view, all the world is indeed a stage and we the actors on it. The only Reality is that which can be found behind sense experience; therefore, gods, demons, being born, dying, dissolving, or levitating oneself are nothing more than a dream from which we can only awaken if we cut the ties that bind us to our senses, our never-satisfied hunger for experience.

What we in the West think of as "magic" (that is, spectacular feats involving self-rising ropes and dancing cobras) has little to do in the long run with the more philosophical side of Taoism, Hinduism, and Buddhism. There are many stages within the laws of Nature, some known and some unknown. What we consider miraculous will no doubt be ho-hum to citizens of the late twenty-first century. To the mystic on his way to Buddhahood, supernatural powers and such are only another nuisance en route. Patanjali, the first great Indian categorizer of yogic experiences, advises his readers to ignore whatever marvelous powers come upon them through their meditative efforts. Tempting as they are, so-called magical powers are as inimical to the final enlightenment as beer and cigarettes.

The goal of the mystic is nothing short of complete union with the One power from which springs every created thing. It is what the Buddhists call gazing into one's own true nature. We tend to cling to events, wishes, or other people, and therefore find little time for setting out in search of our "true natures." The magician has some cockeyed idea of finding *his* true nature through controlling the elements, both seen and invisible. Hindus might say he can't help but act out his *karma* (destined life role) and that, in its own way, magic is this particular man's struggle toward finding himself. He may succeed in calling down a salamander or two, or making lots of money by reading people's minds and fooling them, but in the long run, the magician has gotten no closer to the goal than the fishmonger who couldn't care less about magic *or* mysticism. It's something like trying to survive solely on a diet of candy.

Thus, supernatural events may or may not necessarily occur on the mystic's path. In themselves, they neither enhance nor distract him from his task unless he lets them. Like Buddha, the real yogi examines the unfolding of the *siddhis* (supernormal powers) as mere stages in his development, much as we might reflect on our changing bodies during the process of growing up. Interesting perhaps, but not enough to keep you from moving on to other subjects.

In our Western civilization priests and rabbis and ministers serve as mediators between their congregants and the Divine. Today, their function overlaps with that of doctors, psychologists, and teachers. Nobody goes to a modern clergyman for magical purposes—except for an occasional eccentric Englishman, perhaps, who is looking for someone to exorcise an unhappy poltergeist from his barn. In the East, however, magic and mysticism and religious ritual all overlap. The monk and magician are often one and the same man; the Tibetan *lama* (priest) can be either the saintliest of celibate hermits, mind-focused on God twenty-four hours a day, or the earthiest of merchants who, for a fee, will chart horoscopes, curse his customers' enemies, or blow up hailstorms.

This overlap makes it almost impossible to tease apart the mystics from the magicians, since the superhuman discipline imposed on the monk often leads him as well to superhuman endurance and "powers." Rather than make lists differentiating magicians from mystics, let's just say that the unrelenting mystic finds out about his supernormal possibilities and shuns them. The misguided or overly ambitious yogi remains stuck to magic, often falling into nasty practices and ultimately losing control over everything—like Faust and the Devil. Ramakrishna, the greatest Indian saint of the nineteenth century, compared using magical powers to eating excrement!

AUTHOR'S NOTE: Many of the events, philosophies, and supernormal happenings that will be described in this book are taken literally in the cultures from which they sprang. The Western reader is free to question them from his own logical point of view and training. The author merely presents them as they occurred on their home ground, making no judgments either way.

I gave up all thoughts of this life, because I saw that there is no certainty as to when death may come upon me. . . . But I desire Buddahood in this very lifetime; therefore I am devoting myself to devotion and meditation in such an energetic way.

JETSUN MILAREPA
(A.D. 1051–1135)

ORIENTAL
MYSTICS
&
MAGICIANS

(Overleaf) A stone statue of Brahma dating from the tenth or eleventh century. Brahma is the Hindu god of creation and birth.

INDIA

Holy men come from all classes, but official priests must be born into Brahman (high caste) families. Merely being born a Brahman, however, does not make you holy—or even very religious, for that matter. Much of the caste system is outdated, no longer serving the ancient social function for which it was created. In the first centuries of our era, Indian Brahmans were exclusively priests and scholars. Now it is not uncommon for a Brahman to own a department store. Poor Brahmans often had to go hungry rather than take food from a lower-caste family; but all that is changing now in India. For our purposes, we shall examine the traditional customs and training practices that must be followed if a young Brahman male wishes to enter the mystical priesthood.

Brahmans who wished to attain supernormal powers with the help of spirits spent their time reading and studying the rules in the *Agrouchada Parikchai* (Book of Spirits). By manipulating the sound AUM (Hindu symbol for Creation, Preservation, and Transformation of the Universe) a priest could control all of heaven and earth, the elements, and everyone both around and far from him. This is not as easy as it sounds on paper, for the young man must be willing to sacrifice all normal desires, hopes and activities and devote himself to years of lonely discipline that might take him far from human populations, even to the borders of deprivation and bodily death.

A Brahman boy's birth is immediately noted according to the hour, day, year, epoch, and astrological situation. Nine days later the family celebrates his symbolic initiation by making sacrifice to Vishnu (the Creator) in a ceremony called a *poudja*. The mother, seated on a chair, holds the boy while an officiating Brahman pours water on his head and into the parents' palms. Mother and father drink, and the priest then sprinkles the gathered relatives and friends with the same water. The child's father brings the priest a dish of bronze, or silver, or terra cotta—depending on what he can afford—bearing a betel leaf as a gift. In this way the child is considered purified. Perhaps you have noted, with some familiarity, that the ceremony is a type of baptism. For ten days the mother remains alone in order to purify herself further from the birth process. As Hindus believe that birth into this world is a sign that the soul has not fully transcended its earthly karma, we should not be surprised about this combination of joy and seriousness after a baby is born. Lucky to be a Brahman, and a boy at that! The mother's ten-day isolation period is completed with prayers at a local temple.

Twelve days later, the boy is ready to receive his name. The new father gathers guests in his home, and offers a religious gift to the element fire and to the nine gods ruling the planets. Writing the name of the boy on a wooden tablet containing the child's horoscope, he chants it aloud three times, with all the guests repeating after him:

> Blessed be the name of Brahma. This is my son and his name is "Arjuna." Listen attentively in order that you may remember it.

Followed by the guests, the father goes to the garden and plants a tree while reciting:

> In the name of the powerful and just Brahma, all you who are here present, bear this in mind. This tree is planted on Arjuna's name day, in the third year of the fifth lunar century of the thirtieth divine epoch.

There is a grand feast at the end of the ceremony at which each guest receives an engraved cup with the boy's initials on it. This departing gift is a practical reminder of the child's legitimacy in case of later disputes about his birth. The ancestral spirits are invoked by the officiating priest, who again receives another betel leaf in payment for his services.

At the age of seven months the boy is given rice for the first time. This, too, entails ceremonial ablutions and feasting. The guests sit on a podium decorated with fruit-tree branches, while sacrifices in the form of food are offered to the lunar spirits protecting the family. Women sing and drive away evil spirits that may be lingering over the boy's head. The priest blesses the caste sign (a belt that is bound around the child's loins) and feeds him his first portion of boiled rice. All the company then eat.

When he is three, the child is bathed and braceleted with

coral and sandalwood beads and necklaces. Led by the priest to a spot under a garlanded dais, and surrounded by relatives and guests, the boy is readied for tonsure—his first haircut. The priest offers food or incense to the boy's dead ancestors on both sides of the family. Someone carries in a statue of fertility that has been decked with flowers and fruits and, while the women sing, the barber shaves the head, leaving a lock at the back which is never cut. Once again the women drive away evil spirits; the child is bathed, and food and gifts are offered all around.

Until the age of nine, when he is ready to become a novice, a Brahman boy remains with his mother and the other women in the household. At the end of that period, by taking the sacred saffron-colored thread and placing it around his neck, the young Brahman qualifies himself as a student, or candidate for mystical initiation. His *guru* (teacher) must be a man of sixty or more, who teaches him both the physical and mathematical sciences. When the boy (now considered a man because he wears the sacred thread) reaches sixteen, he is married and entitled to study the occult sciences. Each day while reciting his scriptural readings he must recite the AUM. And from this time forward, he must venerate his teacher as if he were divine. It is not the physical man being worshiped, but the spirit of the divine teacher, Brahma himself, that the student sees in his guru. Most Brahmans only go up to this point. The third degree of initiation—the occult—is reached only by a hardy few. It requires that the candidate eat only once a day (after sunset) and spend all his time in prayer, fasting, and renunciation.

An important symbolic act during the poudja *is the presentation of food and incense to the gods. Only Brahmans may perform the rites.*

The man who accomplishes this phase achieves command over time, space, man, and even death.

Twenty years after the first such initiation, during which the novice has deprived his senses, disciplined his intellect, and strengthened his will by invocation, prayer, and sacrifice, he becomes recognized as a *grihasta* (a householder living in the world, yet retaining control over domestic spirits) or a *pourohita* (a priest of a popular god-cult who can exorcise demons and who is entitled to officiate over ceremonies in homes and temples) or a *fakir* (a magician who manifests his occult powers in public). None of these three types are ever admitted to a second degree of initiation, but rather remain where they are Fakirs, though able to communicate with the highest initiates who may wish to use their powers, never get mystical instruction from a bona fide temple. These men are usually arrested in their spiritual development at the stage of occult exhibitionism. Some have been known to

stand on one leg for twelve years, lie down on nails, and perform other such "significant" acts almost compulsively.

The highest initiate is called a *sannyasi*, holy man. He lives in a temple and rarely appears in public, though his teachings may reach the outside world through oral communication. Twenty years after attaining this noble state, the sannyasi becomes a *sannyasi-nirvany*, a naked hermit who has broken his ties with the earth. These men live in constant meditation (in an elated state called *samadhi*) without sleep or food. Once a week after sunset they emerge from their meditations to eat, and once in five years they appear in public during the grand festival of fire. A French traveler early in the twentieth century describes such an event:

> *They appear like specters, and the surrounding atmosphere is illumined by them by means of their incantations. They seem to be in the midst of a column of light rising from earth to heaven. . . . The air is filled with strange sounds, and the five or six hundred thousand Hindus who have come from all parts of India to see these demigods, as they are esteemed, prostrate themselves flat in the dust, calling upon the souls of their ancestors.*

Of these holy men, seventy Brahmans who have passed the age of seventy are elected to guard the *Law of the Lotus* (the occult science) to prevent it from falling into the hands of the uninitiated. These men must not show anger, nor must they care about life or death, health, or intellectual matters. Thinking only of God, they destroy all sensual desires, all imperfections, and wander the earth, owning only a wooden platter, gourd, earthen vessel, and bamboo basket. So divorced are they from the earth's treasures that their im-

plements may not bear even a trace of precious metal. Who-
ever of them is initiated into the sannyasic stage and informs
anyone on the outside about its secrets is put to death.

After being purified by washing, the yogi covers himself
with ten pieces of cloth. The guru gives him a symbolic
seven-jointed bamboo stick, some lotus flowers and powdered
sandalwood, then whispers the sacred *mantra* (personal invocation) into his ear. At the end of the initiation, the yogi
takes up his stick, drinking bowl, and a gazelle skin which
serves as bed and meditation seat. He smears his body with
ashes, is allowed to eat only a handful of rice once a day
after sunset, must shave his head and face once a month, don
wooden sandals, and live by begging. So strict are the rules
even about obtaining alms, that he must merely stand among
crowds without asking for anything, and must remain content with what he gets—or doesn't. Without either thanking
people or complaining to them, he must stand while eating,
or go on his way if refused. The yogi of this order is so divorced from the world that even the dissolution of empires
cannot concern him. His only purpose in this life is to become enlightened by subduing *all* personal human weak-
nesses.

At night upon returning to the temple, he meditates for
several hours. At this point, he has learned to separate soul
from body, and studies further incantations with his supe-
rior guru. First-degree initiates achieve occult powers through
fasting, mental discipline, and bodily privation. Second-degree
initiates are only a step ahead in their evocations and occult
abilities; while third-degree yogis achieve knowledge beyond
all earthly speculations. Fasting and prayer and isolation have
given them power to make wild beasts as tame as lambs, or to
make rivers overflow and the sun to pale. By sitting naked in
the center of a circle surrounded by continually blazing fires,

they have grown inured to all extremes of heat. By burying themselves to the neck in sand for years, they have learned to die in this life.

Today such extreme mortifications are seen as outrageous even in India. The new brand of initiate remains humble and anonymous, helping his fellow men with his secret knowledge of the human comedy, both present, past, and future. When the sannyasi has passed eighty years of age, he retreats into isolation, taking only the food and water that come to him by chance, and passes away in contemplation of *nirvana* (the Infinite).

Such renunciation is best explained to worldly people like ourselves by example. Take the disciple who asked his teacher for a vision of God.

"Come with me," said the guru, "and I shall show you."

Taking the student to a lake, the guru suddenly pressed the young man's face into the water. After a while he let him go. The student got up.

"How did you feel?" asked the teacher.

"Oh, I thought I would die! I was panting for air!"

"When you feel like that for God," replied the guru, "it won't be long before He appears to you."

The times of day are divided and ruled over by different yogis connected with the temple: noon to sunset is in control of the Master of Philosophy; sunset to midnight is under the direction of the Guru of Evocations, who has all gods and spirits at his command. In the early morning each third-degree initiate must trace a sign on his forehead as a symbol of the highest initiation.

The initiation into yoga of Mahariza, the founder of Jainism.

The design is composed of a circle that symbolizes infinity; there is a border of triangles indicating that everything is subject to trinity; a serpent represents wisdom and stands as a warning to weak minds; finally, there is a seven-knotted stick representing seven degrees of power achieved by evoking spirits. This last power is more important to the yogi than you would think. Evil spirits course through all the worlds and planes of the universe, waiting for vacancies in human bodies. Unwary hermits, novices, and praying sannyasis make perfect hosts for demonic tenants, it seems. This makes it extremely important for the holy man, who is often dangerously perched somewhere between body and soul, to learn the methods of controlling such spirits. To contact them, the yogi must be thoroughly pure in body and mind, alone, and enclosed in a protective circle.

The words or mantras uttered usually match the elements that are inhabited by particular demons—earth, air, fire, water, *akasha* (vital etheric fluid). In the city of Allahabad, noted for its great astrologers and diviners, occultists use the exact hour connected with its elemental counterpart. That is why the Indian seer immediately inscribes the time when he began his invocation down to the last minute. It's a matter of co-ordinating an entire system of planets, demons, elements, and—in the case of evil magicians—sixty-four different kinds of animals, drugs, and bones.

The akasha, according to Indian philosophers, is an unseen vital fluid of sorts that, like electricity, runs invisibly through Nature and (also like electricity) puts all beings in touch with one another. By acquiring control over this powerful element, yogis can influence and manipulate all animate and inan-

Siva, the god of yogis.

imate beings—spirits included. As he purifies himself and un-
tangles the cords of the soul from the gross matter of the
body, the yogi becomes more sensitive to the akashic fluid
and therefore more capable of manipulating it according to
his will.

"Yoga" is literally a "binding" or "yoking" together of
psychic power and spiritual development. By detaching himself gradually from the world, the yogi attempts to bind the
lower powers (residing in the lotus-shaped center at the base
of the spine) with the higher ones that are seated at the top of
his head. All practices ultimately come from three great books of
yoga discipline: *The Upanishads*, Patanjali's *Yoga Sutras*, and
The Bhagavad Gita. Reading these scriptures and determining
to follow this disciplinary course makes one a *sadhak*, or "early
practitioner of the discipline," which is known as *sadhana*. To
this end, the student must find a proper guru, preferably one
who has himself experienced "enlightenment," or the supreme
spiritual wisdom that transcends even the occult powers. It
is the guru, at this first stage, that is most important. Like the
Brahman's initiation, the yogi's may be given through the
guru's whispered words; but unlike the Brahman's closed system, anyone at all can become a yogi, even women—who are
called *yoginis*. One need not be a celibate monk in order to
practice yoga. Some of the greatest yogic saints were married
men and women with families.

The best place to embark on the yogic path is either somewhere in the Himalayas or near the Ganges River, two of the
most sacred places on earth. The yogi's monastery is called
an *ashram*, and, like the Catholic monastery, is set away from
the world, its inhabitants devoting their lives to austerity,
prayer, and meditation. Householder yogis may come for
days, weeks, months, or even years at a time. Great saints

and sages among the yogis are called *rishis;* hence, *Rishikesh* (Lord of the Senses), an Indian city renowned for its great holy men, is revered even today. *Muni* is a saint who has taken a vow of silence and spends his life in meditation, either at an ashram or as a wanderer.

Physical preparation for the mental disciplines required in meditation is called *hatha yoga.* This is the system best known in the West, where "yoga" is almost entirely identi-fied with standing on your head. *Raja yoga* (the "king" of disciplines) is a process whereby the student tries to loosen himself from the grip of his persistent thoughts so that the mind may dissolve gradually into the Truth beyond mind, beyond thought. Abstaining from meat, liquor, tobacco, and other stimulants is supposed to be helpful in sharpening the body, mind, and will. One yogi describes it thus:

> *A man with desires cannot be a yogi. You should not have any desire. Any desire is an obstacle. It will make the mind go out. Now, can you hear anything if it is outside? God is within, and the mind that is without cannot hear or see God. That is the secret of yoga.*

Music has been used as both a disciplinary and an emo-tional form of meditation on the Divine. Krishna, an em-bodiment of the Creator, intoxicated a group of cowherders and maidens with the music from his flute. This is a mythi-cal way of saying that extreme concentration on particular sounds is also a means of transcending one's mundane thoughts. There is even a documented case of an Indian yogi named Nada Brahmananda who can make music of his own body merely by concentrating on certain points from which there issue humming sounds that have an extremely soothing effect on the listener. To produce this mystical-musical effect, the *swami* (celibate monk) studied for ten years with an expert guru-musician and was then initiated into *sannyas* (the religious life) at an ashram. Here he was permitted by his guru to use his music for meditation purposes, and that is how his remarkable gift was discovered. Since Hindus believe that all of Creation was achieved when God uttered the sound AUM, it is not surprising that yogis use the discipline of sound, *nam*, as a means toward making contact with their Lord. To this end, some sects advise repetition of the holy names, or *bhajan*, which is unimpeded concentration on the divine sound current that runs throughout the entire universe.

There is a branch of white magic used by Brahman priests exclusively that follows the teachings spelled out in the *Atharva Veda*, a textbook on immortality, health, love, wealth, and so on. All you need do to live forever is call the right Brahman priest and have him cast this spell:

> *Immortality be upon this one! He is a sharer of the Sun's everlasting life. Indra and Agni have blessed him, and have taken him into immortality. Bhaga and Soma are with him, carrying him high, to prolong his days.*
>
> *There will now be no danger of death:*
> *This world will keep you, forever, rise up! . . .*
> *[and so on].*

This secret work of the Brahmans teaches how to use plants for treating illness, especially the kind brought on by demons. Talismans must come from the *sraktya* tree as wooden

All Indian scripture is guarded over by the Brahman, or priestly, caste. Some schools of yoga recommend the study of scripture as a means to enlightenment.

cuttings that are shaped into the required form—the totem likeness of a lover, a weapon for battle, or a healthy limb. The charm, tied to one's right arm, is carried as a defense against black magic. This is not as literal as it sounds, for the spirits or talismans employed are really viewed by their bearers as symbolic agents for a greater power that the magician has absorbed by concentrating on the particular akashic force embodied in the token.

Certain fakirs spend lifetimes studying this kind of sympathetic magic that depends on a belief in interceding spirit forces. Should the Brahman wish, for example, to suspend the laws of physics, he must call upon the guardian of those laws for help. Only the utmost concentration makes it possible for him to move objects through the air, gather flowers from

Mortification of the body is one of the more simple-minded methods for gaining self-realization. Fortunately, this is going out of style in India today.

out of nowhere, or produce musical vibrations without instruments. Evocation of the spirits can only be accomplished after a life of great worldly sacrifice and asceticism. Only then will he get results from following the instructions in the *Atharva Veda*. Like everything else, it takes hard work to become a professional fakir.

Seated cross-legged on the floor, he does a few breathing exercises and recites the word *yoom* sixteen times. Imagining that his body is melting away, the magician closes his nostrils and holds his breath for as long as he can, thinking the syllable *room* six times. Then he concentrates hard on the particular spirit he wishes to evoke, and pronounces the word *loom* thirty-two times. At this point, the fakir's soul supposedly departs his body for a moment. When consciousness returns, the spirit reveals itself within a small clay model that has been prepared for it in advance. The rites completed, the fakir must leave the trance, reciting *oom* and yoom three, and nine, times, respectively. Now he cries:

> *O mighty spirit of the Pitris! O Great and noble One! I have invoked thee, and thou hast appeared! I have provided a body for thee—a body formed from my very own body. Art thou here? Come, manifest thyself in this smoke [incense]; partake of that which I have offered as a sacrifice for Thee!*

The spirit shape appears in the smoke and accepts some rice. Then it fetches any other spirit the fakir orders, including dead relatives who give advice. The satisfied magician turns out the light; the spirits congregate for a bit and chat. The clever fakir will listen in; this is a fine opportunity for obtaining special information. After the spirits have disbanded, the fakir again lights his lamp and gets up from the floor. Removing the draperies from the windows and doors, he frees the evil spirits he has entrapped there and then sits down to eat. The meal over, he washes his hands and mouth and chews on basil. Later, he must perform some benevolent deed, like giving alms or doing volunteer work.

Great masters among these magicians are said to control all the gods as well as spirits, all heaven and earth. Their power comes from the top, and, because there are no rules for such supermen, they can turn Nature upside down if they wish. Even the stars bow to them.

(Overleaf) The great fifteenth-century founder of the Vaishnava sect, Sri Chaitanya. The artist depicts him forgiving his assailants.

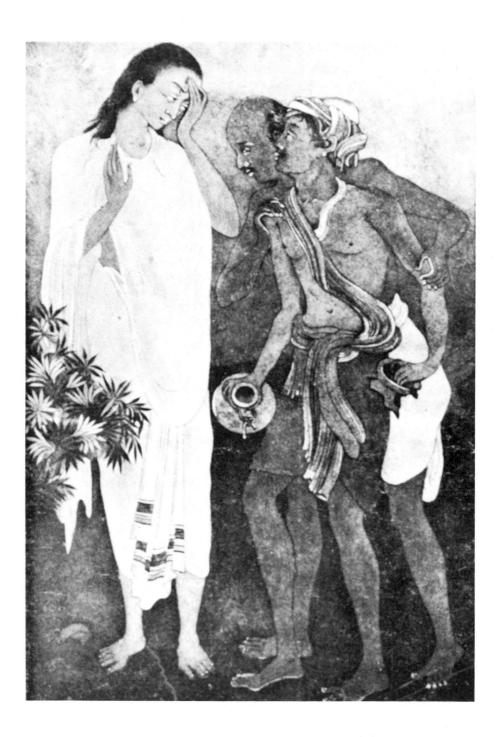

SRI CHAITANYA

The followers of this great Indian saint believe him to be an incarnation of *Krishna* (the Lord) himself. By chanting his holy name, these disciples hope to find self-realization. Again reverting to the yoga of sound, or tuning in to the divine vibration that runs throughout the universe, Chaitanya's disciples work their way through three stages of evolution: life in the material world, the clearing away of the material world, and the transcendental knowledge of the perfect god. By turning all of the senses and desires inside out, that is, away from external objects and toward the idea of Krishna —by means of exercise, yogic breathing, fasting, and sexual abstinence—these celebrators of the divine name divert their lower impulses toward the higher path. Who was the man responsible for creating an entire sect of Krishna followers that influenced millions in India and continues to do so now in the form of Krishna-Consciousness Societies all over the world?

Chaitanya Mahaprabhu was born in Nadia, a small village in Mayapur, India, on the eighteenth of February in 1486 during an eclipse of the moon. His parents were poor Brahmans who looked forward to great things from early on, since the grandfather (an astrologer) had predicted a wonderful spiritual future for the beautiful child. His golden complexion led immediately to his nickname, "Gour Hari," and "Nimai" was added soon after to commemorate his birth near the nim tree. From birth to the age of five, Chaitanya was supposed to have been involved in many wonderful and miraculous events. As an infant, for example, he cried continuously until his mother shouted out: "Haribal!" (the name *Hari* being a variant of Krishna). Then, probably aware of his mission even as a baby, he would calm down. When given candy he would eat clay instead, his reason being that every candy was only "clay transformed." Debating with the child, his mother replied: "Earth, while in the state of a jug, can be used as a water pot, but in the state of a brick such a use is not possible. Clay, therefore, in the form of candy is usable as food and not clay in its other states." Philosophically won over, the boy admitted that he had been silly, and ate his candy. Such was the intellectual nature of his early childhood.

One day a religious Brahman on a pilgrimage was invited into the house. The man cooked and read and prayed, with Krishna always in mind. When he had prepared the sacrificial rice as an offering to the god, the boy came and ate it. Puzzled by the child's daring, the Brahman prepared a second offering, which the boy again ate. A third time the Brahman cooked his rice after all the family had fallen asleep. Now the boy appeared as Krishna to the devout Brahman, and, again taking the rice, gave him his blessing.

Two thieves once tried to kidnap the child in the hope of getting his jewelry. With an offer of sweets, they led him down the road away from home. By exercising an illusion, he managed to lead them right back to his house, frightening them so badly that the thieves just left him on the doorstep and fled.

By the time he was eight years old, Chaitanya was proficient in Sanskrit grammar and rhetoric. After a while he didn't even require a tutor, but read all he needed by himself in his educated father's library. When his brother left to become a monk and his father had died, Chaitanya was elected to stay at home and console his mother. As the new man of the household, it was decided that he be married to Lakshmi Devi, a village acquaintance, at the age of fifteen. Even at this early point in his career, Chaitanya had developed a reputation for scholarship, particularly in philosophy and Sanskrit. As a married man, he was responsible for earning a living, and so went off to the banks of the Padma River to display his great learning in return for payment.

While he was away, Lakshmi Devi was bitten by a snake and died soon after. In typical mother-in-law fashion, Chaitanya's mother prepared for another wife, this time Vishnupriya, the daughter of a Raja *pandit* (wealthy scholar). By now the young man was himself the most renowned scholar in the region. When he was sixteen he had already defeated in debate the greatest pandit of the period, Keshab Misra of Kashmir. It was also around this time that Chaitanya traveled with some of his own students to Gaya, where he was initiated into the spiritual life by Iswara Puri, a sannyasi. This experience marked a turning point for Chaitanya, who thereafter devoted himself to religious matters. So strongly did he preach his new *Vaishnava* (nondualist) faith, that those who knew him from childhood were astonished. No longer was he, Chaitanya, the child prodigy or the sixteen-year-old intellectual, proficient only in dry rhetoric and grammar, but a true holy man, swooning in ecstasy at the name of Krishna and showing divine powers to his fellow scholars in public.

Now remarried, and again expected to earn a living for his household, Chaitanya opened a school where he preached, taught, sang, and danced. Many disciples gathered around him, and soon a larger center was formed in the village of Nadia, to which worshipers and scholars flocked from everywhere in Bengal. To his closest followers he said: "Go, friends, go through the streets of the town, meet every man at his door and ask him to sing the name of Hari with a holy life, and you then come and report to me every evening the result of your preaching."

Of course the devotees met the two worst characters in town the minute they went out. And, as to be expected, they were heartily cursed and insulted for their pains. Within a few days, however, the villains had undergone a miraculous conversion and could be found dancing and singing the name of Krishna in the streets.

The people of Nadia recognized a prophet among them and followed him around in droves as he preached, performed wonders, taught, and sang. By the time he was twenty-three years old, Chaitanya had the entire town singing the name of Hari Krishna throughout the markets, alleyways, and bazaars. Some aristocratic Brahmans protested against his openly ecstatic behavior. The conflict grew until one day a group of his detractors came to his house and, breaking a drum he used in his singing, warned him to either stop his odd religious behavior or convert to Islam. In answer to this, Chaitanya ordered the villagers to appear at night bearing torches. Marching out among them with his religious dancers divided into fourteen groups, he confronted

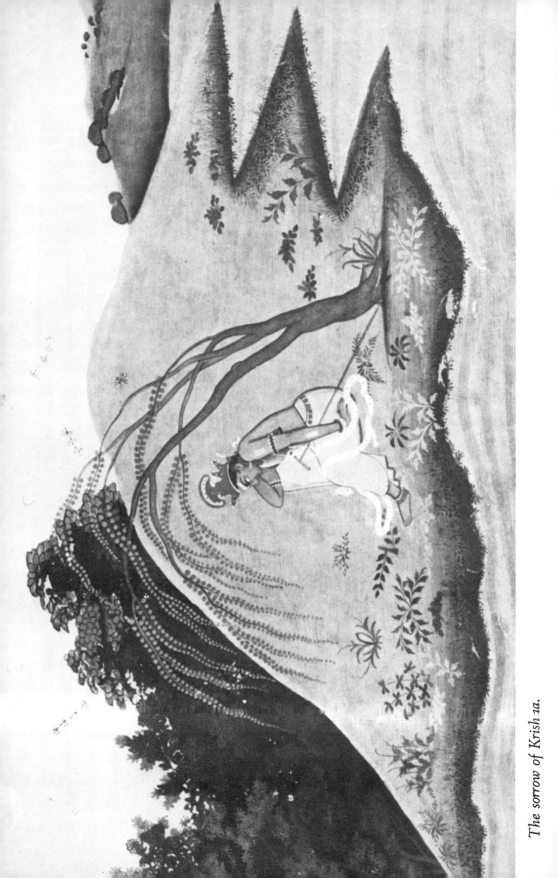

The sorrow of Krishna.

his leading enemy at the door of the man's home. A long conversation ensued. Nothing happened. Then suddenly Chaitanya touched the man's body and the angry Brahman began to weep. Soon he was in ecstasy and had joined the party of dancers. It did not take long after that for the world outside the village to hear about Chaitanya's spiritual power; hundreds of nonbelievers were converted daily, people flocked from everywhere to catch a glimpse of him, to dance and sing the praises of God in his presence.

But again jealous Brahmans tried to block his efforts. This time Chaitanya decided to end all worldly difficulties by becoming a sannyasi himself. Under the guidance of his guru Keshab Bharati, he took his vows at the age of twenty-four. Both his mother and his wife were desolate. Begging him to stay, they clung to his garments—but to no avail. A true holy man, Chaitanya had seen his greater mission, the need to detach himself from *all* worldly relationships for the good of all. He had his head shaven, assumed the cotton cloth, and carried only the hermit's stick and water bowl. In his years of wandering across India, he acquired a vast following, including the greatest scriptural scholar in the country, who became a close and dedicated disciple.

Making his way southward, he cured a leper, caused seven trees to disappear, and converted all those he met to Vaishnavism, the nondualistic faith in a personal God. Even rivals and heretics were swept up in his train. Ascetics in Benares kissed his feet and asked to be blessed. In the jungles he was seen to make elephants and tigers dance at the mere recitation of the name "Krishna."

Chaitanya's wanderings ended when he was thirty-one. At this time he moved into the house of a follower in Puri where, for eighteen years, he preached and taught, always surrounded by many loyal disciples. Then, in his forty-eighth year, Sri Chaitanya disappeared and was never seen again. Was he indeed the god Krishna who, having accomplished his purpose on earth, retired to await still another incarnation a few centuries later? The disciples of Ramakrishna, another great Indian saint, believe so.

(Overleaf) The Buddha.

JAPAN

Contrasting with the hot climate of India, which permits total mendicancy on the part of its monks and yogis, the Japanese setting demands manual labor of Zen disciples. Master Pai-Chang wrote in the eighth century: "If one does not do any work for a day, one should not eat for a day." Although all the yogic rules were originally imported from India along with Buddhism during the sixth century A.D., they naturally assumed the traits of their new followers and were adapted to a new social and intellectual, as well as climatic, environment.

Zen Buddhists are as practical as Indian yogis are otherworldly; novice monks must undergo tests in their monasteries not unlike school examinations. They are hardened by such procedures as being kept waiting for three days in the courtyard of the monastery before being allowed to enter. Then they are placed inside and permitted to do nothing but meditate (*zazen*) under the strict eye of a senior monk. At first all comers are refused entry. Waiting until somebody inside remembers that he is there, sitting on the porch with bowed

head, eating only what they send out to him and immediately resuming his humble posture when he is finished with his meal, the young novice undergoes his *niwazume* (waiting period) with patience. Sometimes, if he is lucky, a senior official will come out and insult him or box him on the ears. Evenings, he will be allowed to meditate in a specially provided meditation area. The next morning, with aching back, he returns to his bowed posture outside. When at last permitted in, he is put on probation and watched carefully for evidence of his dedication and seriousness.

Between December 1 and December 8 (the period commemorating Buddha's enlightenment) Zen monks undergo their harshest meditation course of the year. This is called *robatsu dai sesshin,* concentration of one's mind day and night without the usual intervals. Private meetings with one's *roshi* (master, or guru) are the only socializing permitted during this disciplinary period.

Like yogis in ashrams, Zen monks may go on pilgrimages as wandering beggars at certain intervals in their training. But in Japan there are very definite programs set aside for different seasons and stages in a novice's development. The rules have all been carefully prescribed by enlightened roshis from the past, and are still adhered to. The novice attends lectures on Zen Buddhism, has his head shaved, takes a ritual bath. It would be more interesting, perhaps, to follow the course of a typical day in the monastery.

Rising at three A.M. and moving fast, the monks gargle with water, splash more cold water on their faces, and immediately begin the early-morning scriptural prayer. Then they split off into groups that wish either to speak with the master or to sit in zazen. Breakfast follows, then further meditation, and housecleaning, for which each has an appointed task. Certain days are set aside for lectures and begin from seven A.M. in

These priests on pilgrimage are obviously "singing for their suppers." Zen Buddhists believe in working for their keep.

summer and eight A.M. in winter. Others are devoted to alms-begging; the monks leave the monastery only after they've finished their cleaning chores on these days.

Lunch is served at ten in the morning on lecture schedule, and at eleven when the monks have been out begging alms. The hour after lunch is devoted to zazen in individual, rather than the usual group, sessions. This hour over, manual labor begins: gardening, wood chopping, carpentry, tailoring, and the like occupy the men until three P.M. in winter and four P.M. in summer. Another prayer period follows, and dinner is served at three-thirty or four P.M., depending on the season. Twilight ushers in another zazen session, and the final opportunity of the day for a monk to speak with his roshi about his meditation progress. The day ends at eight P.M., except for the *sesshin* period in December, when the monks do with only three hours of sleep taken sitting up.

Physical training comes from the hatha yoga exercises, all designed to straighten one's posture, quiet the mind, and control the breath. The cross-legged lotus posture is most effective for strengthening the back in order to sit for long periods in zazen, but Zen monks know that it is merely a tool that will ultimately be used for benefiting all human beings, not only themselves. As followers of the Buddha, they practice the discipline of the "Middle Way"—that is, not experiencing too many extremes of heat, cold, starvation, or fullness, hardness or softness. In his search for enlightenment, Buddha was repelled by the cruel ascetic practices of some yogis he came across. Determined to learn every way and follow on every path, he subjected himself for a time to such rigorous methods in the cold Himalayan wastes. When he had finished, he learned what he needed to know—namely, that it isn't necessary to torture yourself into enlightenment. Extreme pain, like extreme pleasure, he decided, distracts us from our true purpose of looking into our true nature. Hence, the "Middle Way."

There are two traditional sects in Zen, the Rinzai and the Soto. Their goal is essentially the same, to gain enlightenment and use the divine wisdom for the benefit of all living creatures; but their methods differ. In Rinzai, monks face each other while meditating; in Soto, they face the wall, with their backs to each other. Both groups keep their eyes open while meditating, with the eyelids cast downward. Both sects indulge in the practice of *kinhin* (walking meditation), so that it is common for the monks to get up after a certain point and begin making their way around the room. Soto monks walk quietly, pacing half a foot length per breath. Rinzai monks trot quickly.

These "regulations" in themselves are unimportant. The issue is not how many trots you take or whether you face your partner or turn your back to him. What counts is the discipline it requires to notice your bodily and mental actions in detail. Once you have focused on the "automatic" gestures, you find that you can control them. From here, you move inside to your thinking processes, learning to apply the same control to the free-floating thoughts in the mind.

Rinzai training advises controlling the mind by counting the breaths while meditating. Soto masters recommend "themeless" zazen (*shikan-taza*), but allow beginners to count their breaths quietly. Southern Buddhist schools teach their students to move the stomach wall in and out while breathing, and to maintain a sharp consciousness of every physical act as they are walking. Thus, the southern Theravada novice would watch and take note of every lifting, stretching, and flexing motion he makes while walking.

Like the yoga of sound, the listening method is used by Japanese monks, too, in the hope that such total concentra-

47

tion will bring them to *satori*, or enlightenment. The goal, as expected, cannot be reached without the assistance of a qualified teacher who can interpret scripture and follow the course of the pupil's meditation. The relationship between master and student is more specifically outlined than that between guru and novice yogi. In Zen there are very definite rules that must be followed, such as: entering the master's room for individual guidance, *nyushitsu sanzen*; or receiving the *koan*, a word puzzle that must be correctly interpreted by the candidate. The most famous of these koans was devised by the Zen master Hakuin in the seventeenth century, and asks: "What is the sound of one hand clapping?"

In his attempt to answer such a koan, the young monk often endures extreme renunciation, lengthy periods of uninterrupted meditation, and sleeplessness. When he feels he is ready to speak, he approaches the master and recites his answer—usually to a shower of verbal and physical abuse. Picture the frightened novice tiptoeing quietly down the corridor to his roshi's quarters, hitting the small bell at the door twice, and humbly bowing his way into the room, prepared for a sound thrashing. There are many known cases of monks who died or sickened in their lifelong search for the proper answer to a koan.

But even here the monk's troubles aren't over. Should the disciple successfully pass this early test, the roshi makes sure that there are further barriers to hurdle. Full enlightenment is never achieved without struggle, but when it comes, it often hits the seeker when he least expects it—like out in the fields when he is cutting crops, or on the road during pilgrimage.

Since the purpose of Zen is to control the mind and the body, the roshis have made it mandatory for monks to earn their own bread and keep. All the monasteries serve a simple diet of vegetarian foods; not even the leftover scraps go to

After practicing extreme asceticism, Buddha decided that the Middle Way was best. He is depicted here at the end of mortification, ready to resume life once again.

waste, since they are used as stock for soup or gravy. Soybeans, seeds, curds, salads and vegetable oils provide needed protein and minerals. Baths are available on the fourth, ninth, fourteenth, and nineteenth of each month. There is a special "bath monk" whose job it is to set up the tubs, assist the others, and do the cleaning up afterward. When he puts out his "bath is open" sign, the entire monastic population lines up outside. The chief priest is first, the second chief next, and so on down the line to the lowliest novice. Before entering, the monks bow before the guardian statue of the bath, Batsudabara, who supposedly gained enlightenment while on his way to the tub. Hot water is provided by fuel from wood chips and other waste material.

After studying under one master for a few years, the *unsin* (probationer) leaves for an extended stay with another tutor. Yet even monks who have studied for many years away from civilization must prove to themselves and their masters that they have truly succeeded in conquering all desires by once again returning to the everyday world and using their wisdom in the service of others.

Japanese occultists are either official Shinto practitioners or "low magic" (*majinai*) followers. Much of their material resembles Western magic, and a good deal is taken from China. The *Norito,* a tenth-century manuscript collection borrowed from Indian and Babylonian rites, forms the lion's share of Shinto magic. Swords and rice are heavily featured in Japan, but there is no such animal as the Devil connected with the Black Art. In fact, Japanese practitioners see either good or evil works as being totally dependent on the mind of the perpetrator. There are no bargains with Mephisto, no soul-swappings in exchange for supernormal power. You either know how to handle the elements and elementals on your own, or you don't dabble in magic.

Spirits (*kami*) are more closely related to the Indian akashic (i.e. refined matter) principle than they are to Western demons. That is, all forms of life—visible and invisible—are manifest and subject to the man of supreme will and concentration. Even trees, with their supposed inherent power, are potential sources for occult manipulations. Individual trees are inhabited by specific spirits which grow angry and vengeful when you hammer a nail into their abodes. Should you succeed in boring through, you will undoubtedly pull out the spirit with the tree sap. And herein lies the magician's opportunity.

Purified and clad in white from head to foot, he asks the annoyed kami to take it all out on so and so—usually an enemy. Japanese magicians, not unlike most, use their art mainly for protection against other magicians, or for promoting love, curing illness, or procuring power and money. Some use the spirit *Shaki*, a specialist in the field, for exorcising demons or counteracting demonic effects on lovelorn husbands and wives.

(*Overleaf*) *A monklike Hakuin is seen meditating here under the tree where Buddha is believed to have been enlightened.*

THE ZEN MASTER
HAKUIN

Although he based his brand of Zen Buddhism on Chinese traditions, Hakuin developed the kind of Zen practice that would appeal more readily to his Japanese countrymen. Removing the aristocratic stamp from his brand of Buddhism and bringing it to ordinary laymen, Hakuin forged two traditions: one, a strict Rinzai monastic discipline allowing for no art or secular literature; the other, a popular, living variety available even to uneducated peasants.

Hakuin was born in 1686 to a lower-class family in Hara, Japan, and died a celebrated monk in January 1769. He grew interested in Buddhism while still young, then lost his faith and turned to nonreligious literature. Well-versed in both Chinese and Japanese works, he was twenty-two when he found himself making pilgrimages to various temples, where he began to experience gradual spiritual inclinations once more. At twenty-four, he followed the master Shoju, then wandered about again from temple to temple, working at Zen

koans, and seeking enlightenment. He returned to the temple
of his native town of Hara when he was thirty-two, and here
devoted himself to teaching and collecting his own band of
disciples. His biographical accounts of his life, though full,
are based on his personal writings. Torei Enji, his disciple,
used much of Hakuin's own account for his definitive life
history of the master. There is little outside material about
him in existence, so we must depend entirely on Hakuin and
his disciple for the story.

Like Chaitanya, Hakuin went through a period of distant
traveling, preaching, and lecturing, gathering support for the
books he wrote, and collecting followers along the way. Unlike Chaitanya, who advised novices only to love God and
call on His name for enlightenment, Hakuin had some very
strong opinions about the means employed. Zen meditation,
to him, demanded extraordinary faith, doubt before confront-
ing the koans (spiritual riddles), and unwavering persever-
ance. Seeing into one's own true nature (kensho) became his
watchword: the Mu koan and "The Sound of One Hand
Clapping" became his favorite puzzles to enlightenment. Both
these koans—the second of which Hakuin created himself—
were given to his students as subjects for meditation. The
novice must ponder the story of a monk who asked his
master Chao-Chou, "Does a dog have Buddha-nature?" and
was answered with only one word: "Mu!" Under the guidance of his teacher, and with long meditation on the koan, the
student will come to a point where, as Hakuin describes it,
"within his heart there is not the slightest thought or emotion,
only the single word Mu . . ."

As for the "sound of one hand," Hakuin says:

> Five or six years ago I made up my mind to instruct
> everyone by saying, "Listen to the Sound of the

Single Hand." I have come to realize that this koan is infinitely more effective in instructing people than any of the methods I had used before. . . .

What is the Sound of the Single Hand? When you clap together both hands a sharp sound is heard; when you raise the one hand there is neither sound nor smell. . . . There is something that can by no means be heard with the ear. If conceptions and discriminations are not mixed within it and it is quite apart from seeing, hearing, perceiving, and knowing, and if, while walking, standing, sitting, and reclining, you proceed straightforwardly without interruption in the study of this koan, then in the place where reason is exhausted and words are ended, you will suddenly pluck out the karmic root of birth and death and break down the cave of ignorance.

The successful meditator will eventually come to hear the sound of Buddha, ghosts, demons, the sounds of all heaven, earth, hell, the universe. Only meditation on the koan, and an occasional interview with the master, can aid in working it out properly. To this end, Hakuin insisted on the koan as a form of strict spiritual discipline in the midst of activity. It was he who instituted the practice of "walking meditation," in which the monk walks without being aware he is walking and sits without any awareness of being seated because he is wrapped in the mantle of the koan.

His advice to laymen, however, is often quite different. Like all shrewd mystic masters, Hakuin knew that not everyone is inclined or, indeed, even ready for meditation and the contemplative life. Thus, he tells a warrior who writes asking him for instruction, to remain physically strong all of his days. In fulfilling the obligations of a fighter (his karma, in other words), the warrior must be properly groomed and ordered, swords and all. Riding on his horse to meet his enemies head on, he must be so unafraid that he appears to be headed for a "place empty of people." *His* meditative facial expression must be one of valiant ease. Should he follow this advice, he will do in a month what it takes a monk a whole year to accomplish. "In three days he can open up for himself benefits that would take the monk a hundred days." It's all a matter of following the right path.

To common folk, therefore, Hakuin recommends reciting religious formulas designed to prolong life and bring about miracles. At the same time, he acknowledges that this is for "people of inferior and mediocre [spiritual] talents" and resembles more closely the Pure Land school of Buddhism, which advocates calling the Buddha Amida for enlightenment on one's deathbed. Zen, more rigorous, demands efforts on one's own part. Miracles are involved with this world of illusions and have nothing really to do with gazing into one's own nature. Yet not all people are equally equipped to do so. When he does find such a person, as in the case of one wealthy young aristocrat, Hakuin advises that the man abandon entirely his income and the luxuries of his class, and that he "clean up the garden, change the water in the basins, and with a laughing face wash the feet of your retainer's horses."

For nervous breakdown (which he himself is believed to have suffered at the age of twenty-nine), he recommends reciting religious formulas and practicing a form of meditation called *naikan,* which is similar to meditating while performing activity. Practicing Zen when one is sick is advantageous because you are then unburdened of daily work. The only good reason to stay healthy and live long is to use the time for Zen practice.

The Buddha Amida represents the Pure Land Buddhist school, which relies on gods for assistance. Zen demands total self-reliance.

Hakuin had no patience for other varieties of contemplation, and he did not care much for anyone who disagreed with him. A rather moody man, he used his painting and calligraphic ability to draw caricatures, write poems, and illustrate mottoes; in some cases he employed his talents in tearing down other schools of Zen. He must have had a powerful personality, for all teachers in monasteries and temples of Rinzai Zen continue to follow his methods even today.

Hakuin came to his theory of koan meditation through much trial and error, having believed at first in the tranquil, or nonactive, kind. Many attempts failed: "Trivial and mundane matters pressed against my chest and a fire mounted in my heart. . . . My manner became irascible and fears assailed me. Both my mind and body felt continually weak, sweat poured ceaselessly from my armpits, and my eyes constantly filled with tears. My mind was in a continual state of depression." Meeting fortuitously with the hermit teacher Hakuyu, Hakuin learned a secret method of meditation which sent him on to greater success. Difficult koans now became clear, and: "Even though I am past seventy now my vitality is ten times as great as it was when I was thirty or forty. My mind and body are strong . . . I find no difficulty in refraining from sleep for two, three, or even seven days, without suffering any decline in my mental powers. . . . I am convinced that all this is owing to the power gained from practicing this method of introspection."

"This method of introspection" is neither active nor passive, but combines elements of both. Hakuin tells us that he tried cutting himself off from the world as a young man. But even after many years of living as a monk, he had not yet come to see his own true nature. Describing his first spiritual inclinations, he recalls himself as a boy of eight who was brought by his mother to a temple where he listened to a sermon on hell.

The master who called Hakuin a "hole-dwelling devil" might have looked like this priest who is flanked on both sides by wary disciples.

So real were the wails, the flames, and the human suffering to the boy that, when he returned home and sat in the bath, he experimented with the hot water, increasing the heat until his skin prickled. Then, letting out a "cry of terror that resounded through the neighborhood," he resolved to dedicate his life to freeing himself from the bonds of the body. By the time he was fifteen, he had become a monk. Day and night he prayed and studied, and grew increasingly depressed at the emptiness of his search. At nineteen he began to feel that perhaps all of Buddhism was a fraud.

At twenty-two he left for the province of Wakasa, where, while listening to a series of lectures, he achieved his first spiritual awakening. "I concentrated night and day on the Mu koan without a moment's rest, but to my great disappointment I was unable to achieve a pure and uninvolved state of undistracted meditation. Equally disappointing to me was the fact that I could not achieve the state where waking and sleeping are the same [samadhi]." Hakuin persisted, meditating without sleep, without food or social life. "It was as though I were frozen solid in the midst of an ice sheet extending tens of thousands of miles. A purity filled my breast and I could neither go forward nor retreat. . . . I was out of my mind and the Mu alone remained."

One day at the sound of the temple bell, Hakuin found himself transformed; he had broken through the ice and shattered his disbelief. Now he knew truly that all was illusion, even birth and death, even enlightenment, even the koans themselves. Arrogantly, he approached the master Shoju.

"You poor hole-dwelling devil!" cried Shoju. "Do you think somehow that you have sufficient understanding?" And he presented him with still another impenetrable koan. Hakuin pondered the new koan for a long time; when he thought he had found the answer, he again approached Shoju. And again he was greeted with "You poor hole-dwelling devil!" Frustrated almost to the point of quitting, Hakuin found himself in town one day, begging for food. Approached by a madman who was attacking him with a broom, he immediately penetrated through the koan. This time when he returned with his answer to the master, Shoju did not call him a hole-dwelling devil, but merely chuckled. Hakuin went on and progressively experienced three further "enlightenments."

A pilgrimage was the setting for even greater development: passing through southern Ise in a rainstorm, he was soaked to the skin and surrounded by water up to the knees. Suddenly he found himself overwhelmed by bliss and understanding. And he began to laugh so loudly that pedestrians thought he was insane. Still later, in a monastery where he was staying, Hakuin experienced samadhi (satori, in Zen) during walking meditation. From then on, he was established in his perfect knowledge, serene in his discovery of his own "Buddha nature."

Rounding out his life, Hakuin comments on his struggle: "I wish that everyone would realize that studying Zen under a teacher is not such a simple matter after all. Although I am old and dissipated, and have nothing of which I can be proud, I am aware at least I have not spent forty years in vain. . . ."

(Overleaf) Shou Lao, Taoist god of longevity, is surrounded by long-lived animals.

CHINA

In pre-revolutionary China people of all classes believed in
some form of spirit phenomena, usually through the medium
of Lao-tse, a mystic born about 570 B.C., whose *Book of the
Tao* completely transformed the face of Chinese philosophy.
The general pattern of the occult world, for the Chinese
(and Japanese) believer, reads like a ladder map whose apex
is the Supreme Intelligence, and whose descending rungs feature angels, planet spirits, and spirits of the dead. This basi-
cally magical scheme fit in nicely with Lao-tse's Taoist system,
which combined much of Buddhism with the indigenous occult practices of China's Shintoists. Confucian rationalists,
however, took every opportunity to decry the Taoist philosophy. Lao-tse, as Imperial librarian, had access to many ancient and secret books. Thus, he formulated his own beliefs
from a welter of Shinto magical texts, with a little Buddhism
thrown in for good measure. Unfortunately, he could not control those who came after him, nor could he explain person-
ally what he meant by such terms as "the power of the Tao"
or "the secrets of the Tao"; and most disciples took him
literally, using his work as a vehicle for conjuring spirits.

Confucians have nothing to do with Taoism; Buddhists maintain a safe distance from its occult rites, and even its mysticism doesn't attract them much.

Tao magic is, oddly, more closely related to European sorcery than it is to Indian magic, and features similar willow wands, wax dolls, water-divining techniques, and magic mirrors. It is possible that these influences were brought to Europe from China through Arab traders—nevertheless, ideas about obtaining success and power from mirror spirits came our way through Chinese magic.

Taoist magicians compelled the demon to appear reflected in his true shape. Once this was accomplished, its restrictive power over the mirror's owner ceased. One man is said to have become emperor as a result of owning and using such a magic mirror. Any old mirror won't do. Authentic ones are decorated with a unicorn figure, animals representing the four sides of the universe, and other metaphysical creatures. Each magician-priest inscribed the mirror himself so that, "Whenever the sun shines on this mirror, the ink of those inscriptions permeates the images which it reflects, so that they cannot possibly show any false shapes."

One Wang Tu used a magic mirror in A.D. 606 to reflect a mysterious girl who begged him not to kill her after informing him that she was a thousand years old, a refugee from a demon who had once been her boss. Deciding that she had undergone a sufficient number of adventures, she committed suicide by drinking wine, turning into her true shape—a vixen—and dying. For obvious reasons, mirrors like Wang Tu's must be kept covered when not in use.

These three Chinese votive trees, not money but talismans in the shape of money, were made to be offered to the gods.

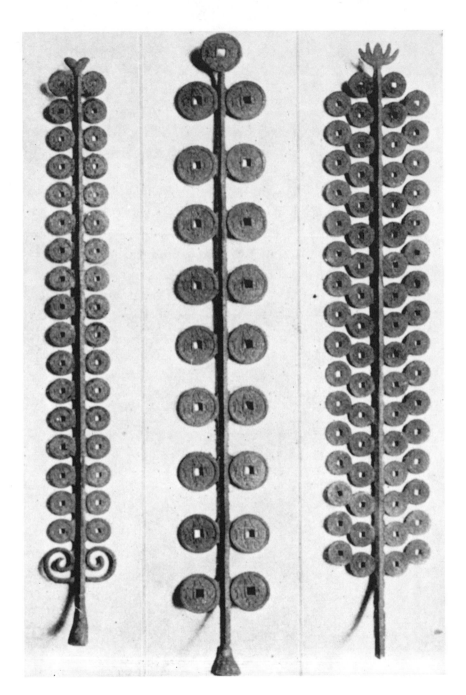

Chinese magicians also use charms. Koh Hung, a fourth-century occultist, author of the *Pao Poh Tsze,* advises on written charms for the traveler, who must be especially wary of mountain spirits. The ink used must be made of a combination of red cinnabar and paint; the pen, of peachwood. Talismans written and blessed by Taoists are so strong that they can scare off wild animals and bandits as well as ghosts and goblins. Some are written in the form of five arrows, presumably poison ones. The script is called *thunder writing,* or *celestial calligraphy.*

Women acquire their fortunes through the use of gold and silver triangles projecting two swords from each base angle. Their charms are always placed on red or yellow paper in red or black ink. Then they are either pasted on a door or bed, or worn in the hair, or hung on a string around a button. Some eager devotees, anxious for more immediate results, may even go so far as to burn the talisman, mix the ashes with tea or water, and then drink it! Influences are believed to enter the body quickly this way.

Like Tibetan lama-magicians (whom we'll discuss more extensively later), Taoists enjoy raising thunder and storms. In China this is accomplished by means of spells and symbols.

Happier symbols designed to bring peace and prosperity are flashed in the faces of demons that bring illness and other misfortunes. Since the sun and moon are especially powerful in combating evil influences, they too are called upon. Light and fire are two more favorites, while the symbol of the East, repeated over and over again, is most potent in bringing down the healing rays of the sun, which rises in the East.

The "all powerful" seal of Lao-tse himself is worn by psychic mediums and supposedly brings them good fortune. So potent is this sign that it can even bring about opposite wishes at once.

Each Taoist sign stands for a specific god. Chang Tao Ling, founder of the cult, is one of the most powerful of these superhuman beings. The leading priests *must* come from his family line, whose seat of power lies in the Kwang-sin department of Kiangsi province. That is why *"chang"* is used more frequently than any other word in Taoist spells. *Shen* or *ling* are used as substitute characters for the names of the gods themselves. If a magician wants a lot of power fast, he might crowd together a group of sympathetic followers whose multiple concentrations will make things happen faster. The larger the group, the stronger the force, is a basic tenet of magicians all over the world. If there aren't any large, willing groups available, the Taoist may express his wish in writing. The written word is extremely powerful to the Chinese magician—especially so since each word is represented by its own picture. Thus, *hiao* or *wao*, when written on paper, depict "shouting by many mouths." The charm must be inscribed only when the sorcerer is concentrating deeply on a powerful god. Experienced Tao-

This charm is typical of those worn by Taoists to ward off spirits or bring good fortune.

ists can get results by merely drawing the characters in the air with their fingers.

> *A sample spell: "Heart of Heaven, eyes of Heaven, core of Heavenly light, defeat the spiritually power-ful light of the earth, sun, and moon, produce your light; quick, quick, let the Law and the command of the Five Emperors be obeyed."*

The *I Ching* (*Book of Changes*) works along similar lines. Essentially a fortune-telling device, the book contains a cer-tain number of ideograms (picture words) taken from Nature: sky, water, mountain, powerful emperor, and the like. The diviner must throw bamboo sticks, or coins, and note down the sums gathered from each of the six castings. Then he con-sults the book, which contains the matching number of lines and fortunes for each possible combination of tosses. It takes a clever diviner, however, to figure out the often inscrutable advice. Still, many people in the West today swear by the Chinese *Book of Changes*.

Koh Hung wrote a number of works describing the feats of Ming Ch'ung-yen, a T'ang dynasty sorcerer, and Kiai Siang, magician in the court of the King of Wu. When the latter asked for a fish dinner, the sorcerer dug a pit, filled it with water, and caught a fish. Then the king hungered for ginger from the faraway Szechwan province. Kiai Siang, always will-ing to please, inscribed a charm and sent it off with a courier, who was told to close his eyes and ride away. The man im-mediately found himself in Szechwan, where he bought the

On the left is Lu-small Sing, Taoist god of honors, and on the right is Han Hsiang Tzü, one of the eight immortal Taoist gods.

ginger. Closing his eyes again, he found himself at the court of Wu just in time to spread the ginger on the cooked fish.

Magicians who indulge in automatic writing use peachwood pencils that come from twigs growing along the eastern sides of trees. Formulas are read before these twigs are lopped off: "Magical pencil, powerful one, each day bearer of subtle power, I cut thee, to tell all." The words must be cut into the tree bark at the opposite side; then the phrase "Wondrous Revelation of the Heavenly Mysteries" is carved below. Set into a six-inch piece of wood, and placed into the hands of a chosen medium, the pencil will be used by a spirit working through the human form. All invited guests must be dressed in white; after having fasted and bathed, they sit at two long, parallel tables. One acts as an altar, covered with goblets of wine, sweets, and fruit. The other is scattered with sand, which will act as a kind of blackboard upon which the pen will write. Everything must be prepared before nightfall. The magician writes one of his prayer charms asking for permission of the "Great Royal Bodhisattva." Giving directions is an important part of the rite, for the spirit must be told the exact location of the house and the name of the person making inquiry. Otherwise, he might lose his way.

The charm and some gold paper are then burned before the altar of the chosen deity. Back at home, the inquirer must write his name and address on a second card which is affixed to his door. At night the other participants go to the door, where they burn more gold paper and bow in welcome to the spirit. He is conducted inside to a ceremony which includes lighting candles and incense and pulling up a chair for him.

Taoist divinities in an eighteenth-century Chinese painting.

At this point, the medium with the pencil goes to the sand blackboard and rests the twig handle on his hands, letting the end graze the sand. The magician chants: "Great Spirit, if you have arrived, please write 'arrived' in the sand on this table."

Then the pencil writes, while the rest invite the spirit to sit—along with the god who supposedly ushered him down, who is offered another seat. All bow before the empty chairs and present the invisible guests with wine and a little more of that gold paper.

"Great Spirit," continues the sorcerer, "what was your august surname, what your honorable name, what offices did you hold, and under which dynasty did you live on earth?"

The spirit traces the answer with the magic pencil. The guests write their specific questions on paper and burn them all together with a strip of the gold sheet. All answers are given separately in the sand. When the spirit has said enough, he traces, "I have finished." Sometimes he may answer in verse, at other times he can be confused in his speech. Odd answers are unscrambled after further tracings and closer study. When one of the party has hit on the right solution, the spirit writes "That is right" in the sand. Each tracing re-quires that the sand be "erased" in preparation for the next question. Anyone who asks a silly question or a disrespectful one is scolded in no uncertain spirit terms.

The medium balances his pencil between the palms of his hands and thanks the spirit for his help. To his praise of the spirit's eloquent language, the medium usually gets the modest reply of, "Nonsense." After midnight, like Cinderella, the

Presenting food to the spirits of the dead is an essential part of the Taoist automatic writing ceremony.

spirit must leave. The party coaxes him a little, but not too much, for fear of angering him. "If there was any want of respect, or attention, Great Spirit," they say, "we entreat thee to forgive us this sin." Then they escort him to the door, burning gold paper all the while. With bows and best regards, they bid him farewell.

Mediums are often chosen at random. But the interpreters of the writing are held in high repute. It takes a very special breed of Taoist to interpret the scratchy pictographic scrawls made by hurried spirits.

The art of devil dancing is practiced by both professionals and amateurs. Ordinary people who are driven into a frenzy by evil spirits find themselves whirling around in trance states.

Those who purposely work themselves up into a frenzy are magicians who are trying to divine some answer or other from the spirit world. Often, Chinese families call upon these devil dancers to gain the solution to problems. It doesn't matter how you induce the spirit to come down, what counts on these occasions is that your magic is powerful enough to catch him, keep him around for a while, and pry the necessary information out of him without losing your life in the process. No doubt, devil dancing is a wilder way of performing than automatic writing or spell-casting. But it, too, requires its own ritual, during which the dancers prepare first with a whiff of incense and a feast. The gathered company is advised to concentrate on the important question. (Recall the extra-special power of a concentrating group of people.)

The host apprises the dancer of the necessary information surrounding the case. Also included here are a band of musicians bearing drums, bells, cymbals, and so on. These start up a song—at first slow and quiet, until gradually they work up the pace to a fever pitch that accompanies the dancer's increasingly faster whirling. More incense is lighted while the dancer now enters into a pattern of fancy footwork. Suddenly he stops short and falls to the floor. This procedure typically runs for fifty minutes against a backdrop of total silence from the spectators. The dancer rises in trance. And now the questions are thrown at him one by one. A scribe comes to the center of the circle and quickly notes down the rapid-fire answers that the spirits are sending through the dancer-medium.

Painted representations of the spirit or god evoked must be pasted on the door of the caller's house. This one is the god of wealth.

Each devil dancer requires his own kind of banquet and ceremonial trappings. Some are in such great demand that they refuse to do house calls but have a flourishing office practice instead. Others demand large gifts; it all depends on the province they happen to work in. Most feared and worshiped of the lot are male and female devil dancers from Manchuria, who are considered specialists without peer in the trade.

Taoist priests are initiated according to their areas and levels of specialization against a set of rules and regulations prescribed by a book of the *Li Ki* series. *Wu* (magicians) fall into the following categories: soothsayer, exorcist, theurgist, or sacrificer. Both men and women are permitted to be priests, though most positions are inherited and passed down from parent to child. Few Wu make themselves known to the public; rather, their clientele seek them out through word of mouth. Their titles are "honorable sir" or "Wuist Master." The initiation procedure is officiated by a nonfamily Wu; and, like novices in other sects, Taoists also must undergo certain stages of trial. Seven days before the actual ritual begins, the candidate must remain isolated in a cell, abstaining from fish, meat, onions, leeks, and garlic. Alcohol is forbidden as well. For the entire period he remains celibate and washes himself frequently while repeating many invocations and prayers.

The last day of his retreat marks the initiation. Three days before this, offerings have been presented to the idols in the Taoist temple. At the appointed hour the initiate enters the shrine dressed all in white, barefoot, and wearing on his head an emblem of the sun. Since he must not touch the ground with his feet as he approaches, he has been carried by one or two assistants from his cell. If for any reason he does touch ground, all the power he has gathered will leave him and fall into the earth.

A Chinese monk stops in a doorway.

Inside the walls of the temple, the chief priest sprinkles rice and water and charms everywhere as he questions the candidate about his readiness to leave the material world. After the novice has answered "yes" to all the questions, he must climb a sword ladder to the background music provided by cymbals, drums, and a buffalo horn. Although the swords are not really terribly sharp, he has successfully completed his "ordeal" and can call himself a true priest of the order at the completion of his ascent. Finally, the novice must approach the altar, ring a bell and announce to the gods that he is now a full-fledged Wu.

What does he use in his new profession? Swords and daggers for exorcism, mostly. Weapons made of peachwood and *kiens* (double-edged daggers) are best at squelching demons. Great warriors' relics also possess much power, particularly if their hilts are wrapped in red cloth. When idle, these swords are put away and carefully slipped into silken cloths. Amulets made of miniswords are worn to keep off demons, but they are only effective if cut from willow wood on the fifth day of the fifth month, when the sun is highest. If a willow has been struck by lightning, it's even more effective.

The Wu may advise his customers to hang such swords at their doors, or carry them at their sides after decorating them with red tassels. In Chekiang the people consider mulberry-wood swords so powerful that even the most diabolical magician, they believe, can be felled immediately at the first shake.

Some swords are made of coins and prove valuable for all occasions. Chinese coins, which have holes in the center, are believed to resemble the hilt of a sword anyway; thus, a group of coins formed into a sword provides strong protection.

This seventeenth-century painting shows a group of scholars studying the Ying-Yang symbol, a masculine-feminine nature sign of the Taoist philosophy.

(Magic frequently assumes that when something resembles something else, there is latent power in a combination of the two. Besides, everyone knows about the power of money.)

Here is an example of the type of spell a Taoist Wu might inscribe on his sword: "I willed the large sword of heaven to cut down specters in their five shapes; one stroke of this divine blade disperses a myriad of these beings."

There are even swords that can do the job by themselves. One Taoist used such an automatic sword to kill demons. He merely put the weapon in an empty room, spat water on it, and angrily ordered it to strike at the spirits. Keeping the door closed for an entire day, he re-entered to find the whole floor stained with blood.

The Wu are recognized by their *kang-i* (red garment). This is the favorite robe worn on ceremonial and magical occasions. It also makes them easy to spot, so that Confucius' followers could rail against them in public as evil heretics. Even the Wu's robe is symbolic in that it is embroidered with trees, mountains, thunder spirals, and dragons to signify his control over all of Nature. Made of a square sheet of silk with a slit in front and a head hole in the center, the robe is sleeveless, and has a wide blue silk border sewn at the bottom. Thick silken ribbons hang down the front. Though it is exactly the same as another robe called "Gown of the Universe," the kang-i is kept aside for more important rituals. Still, Gowns of the Universe are just as liberally embroidered with dragons, eight-sided figures, and tortoises.

In performance, the Wu's hair is piled up on his head and covered by a round cap. Attached to the black cap is a Golden Apex which represents the sun's rays. The rules about these appurtenances must be followed scrupulously, for unofficial clothing does not conduct the magical vibrations.

A Taoist priest robe inscribed in the eleventh year of Ch'ien Lung's reign (1746), made for the head of a Taoist monastery.

A Taoist begging monk.

Female Wu are particularly adept at trances and mediumship. A spirit named Lady Tzse is most popular with female magicians; she has co-operated with them for centuries. Her principal gift has been the bestowal of great literary talent. This is not too hard to comprehend, since much of classical Chinese literature comes from isolated women at the Imperial Court. Lady Tzse's other sidelines are medicine and foretelling the future. The Wu conjure her through a living medium or a doll that will reply to questions. This is accomplished in the following way:

On the fifteenth day of the first month, the women paste a door charm on a strainer and then draw a human face on it. Willow branches make up the limbs; then the strainer is dressed in clothes. The group calls upon Lady Tzse, placing incense and food before her effigy. Suddenly the doll grows heavy. The women now know that the spirit has arrived, and ask away. Most claim that she has answered them. The female Wu of Amoy create special all-purpose images that will function whenever needed, answering every type of question imaginable on all occasions. Presumably, they manufacture these dolls on a large-scale basis and market them to trusted customers.

(Overleaf) The greatest tulku of them all, the Dalai Lama (center) was not only the spiritual king of the Tibetans, but head of state as well.

TIBET

Known variously as "The Land of the Snows" or "Shangri La," Tibet affords us our richest, most colorful view of Eastern mysticism and magic thus far. Its Buddhism, imported wholesale from India in the early part of the Christian era, was grafted onto a primitive, animistic faith known as *Bön*. What often emerges in studies of Tibetan mysticism is a conglomeration of Indian Tantric practices (magical means to mystical ends), pure idealistic Buddhism, and downright black magic.

Lamas—Tibetan priests—often perform simultaneously as exorcists and heads of monasteries because they see no discrepancies in the magical-mystical life. Unlike Indian yogis who have reached the highest plateaus in meditation and who therefore scorn *any* action that might incur rebirth or karma, the Tibetans dwell in many worlds at once. Therefore, it is wise not to draw hard and fast lines between mystics and magicians in that complicated land. Certain practices will repeat themselves both in our discussion of legitimate novices studying in monasteries, and in the activities of self-made lamas too. Remember only that the first group is sanctioned by the official Buddhist clerical hierarchy, and that the second isn't.

The Tibetan system ranks the *Tulkus* ("Living Buddhas" incarnate) at the peak of the monastic pyramid. All other ordained priests are called lamas. The incarnate Buddha that heads the entire system is called the *Dalai Lama;* he performs both as spiritual chief of Tibet and head of state. Student monks are called *trapas.* These officiate largely at funerals, receiving food and gifts in payment. Sorcerers—usually remnants of the Bön sects—are called *ngagspa,* and form the strongest social competition for the officially recognized lama. These ngagspas wear their hair long and are thus recognized as seekers of salvation by means of the Short Path, the way of magic. The ngagspa is easily recognized by his costume: a crown, a 108-rosary-bead necklace made of skulls, an apron of carved human bones, and a ritual dagger (*phurba*) in his belt. You wouldn't want to meet him on a dark night.

No group of Tibetan yogis—be they ngagspas, lamas, or otherwise—are vegetarians. Perhaps it has something to do with the cold weather and scanty supply of vegetables; Tibetan mystics, like ordinary citizens, subsist almost entirely on yak meat, barley, and yak dairy products like milk and butter.

Lamas may dwell on mountain heights in solitary caves called *gompas,* or they may cluster together in monastery gompas. *Lhakhangs,* temple-affiliated monasteries, are called homes of the gods. Many *gomchens* (mystic lamas) are married and surround themselves with gold and silver, lavish

No Tibetan ngagspa *would be caught dead without his apron of human bones.*

jade altars, tombs, and ritual implements. Gomchens enjoy a reputation for quelling demons and causing supernatural events through their lonely contemplations. Within the group are a number of specialists in the art of *tumo*, the generation of body heat. Tibetan winters are long and cold, so that tumo is something most novice monks wish to learn fast. The costume of the expert in the field consists of a long white skirt, wide-armed maroon coat, yellow shirt, coral-bead rosary and earrings.

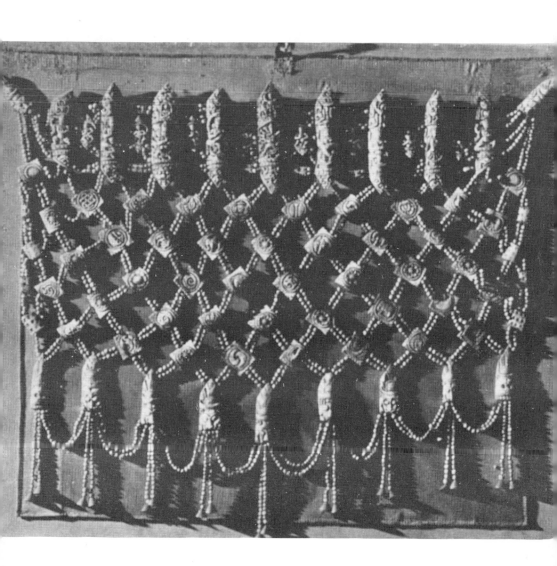

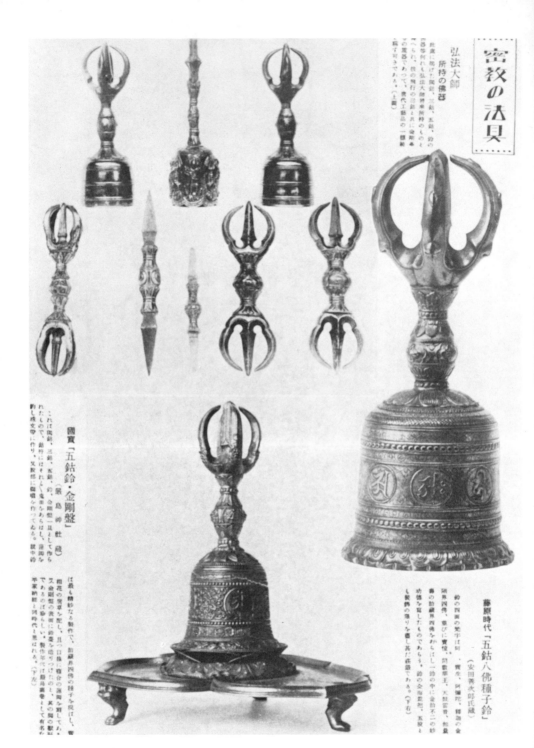

密教の法貝

弘法大師
所持の佛器

此處に揭げた獨鈷、三鈷、五鈷、鈴の四器等何れも弘法大師將來所持のものと傳へられ、他の飛行の三鈷と共に金剛峯寺の寶器であつて、唐代工藝品の一部を窺ひ得きれる。（上揭）

國寶「五鈷鈴・金剛盤」
（嚴島神社藏）

これは獨鈷、三鈷、五鈷、鈴、金剛盤一具として作られたもので、飾付にはそれ〴〵の象を示しあらはし、蓮瓣を釣り残す如く作り、又散間に蓮瓣を作つてゐる。就中の相花の寶珠を配し、且つ口根に複合の蓮閣を設してゐる金剛盤の表面に彫り付けられ、其の彫の麗はしさであるのは珍しい。製作の年代は鎌倉最盛とては最も精妙なる製作で、飾縺共四佛の種子を佩はし、實は最も精妙なる製作で、飾縺共四佛の種子を佩はし、卒塔婆納經と同時代と思はれる。（下左）

藤原時代「五鈷八佛種子鈴」
（安田善次郎氏藏）

鈴の四面の梵字は胎、金、寶生、阿彌陀、釋迦四佛、並に實愛、閻閦菩薩、天鼓雷音、妙金剛界四佛、意に賓愛、閻魔羅王、天鼓雷音、妙の金鈴界四佛を示しあらはし、一鈴の中に金胎不二の妙功德を寫したものであらう、鈴の金胎龍紋、五鈴と も飾の彫り方を整し其だ在意であかる。（下右）

Meditation seats (*gamti*) are square boxes from twenty-five to thirty inches long, the higher side forming a back rest. Lamas throw a cushion on the bottom of the box, where they sit down in the traditional cross-legged posture. A meditation rope (*sgomthag*), usually a woolen sash, is passed under the knees and behind the neck, or behind the knees and back, to keep the meditator awake and upright.

The daily monastic routine might run as follows:

Eight hours of meditation divided into four periods of two hours. Eight hours of study and labor. Eight hours of sleep, eating, and free time. The monks are awakened at three A.M. by reveille, which takes the form of a monk striking on an enormous wooden castanet. All meet and meditate in the great hall. After meditation, a breakfast of rice and unflavored boiled vegetables, or barley tea, might be served against a generally silent background. At midday there would be a morning assembly, featuring monastic dignitaries, including the *Tsogs chen shalngo* (elected ruler of the gompa), who will appear in all his gold and bejeweled finery.

The scene consists of a thousand or more shabby, shaven-headed monks seated on the floor of an enormous *tsokhang* (hall) from whose high ceiling and galleries hang magnificent scrolls depicting countless Buddhas and gods. The walls are covered with paintings of other saints, *tulkus*, demons. Behind rows of butter lamps there are portraits of former monastery officials, and statues that contain their ashes. High lamas sit on thrones, gazing down at the cross-legged multitude below. Lower-ranking priests sit on a descending row of benches. The deep, slow chanting begins against a clamor of

These are only a few of the official instruments used by lamas working with spirits.

bells, oboes (*gyalings*), and trumpets (*ragdongs*). Drums beat out the time in a persistent rhythm that keeps each novice mindful of the whiplash awaiting him at the hands of his *chöstimpa* (sergeant-at-arms) should he move or feel inclined to fool around a bit.

At intermission, tea with butter and salt is· ladled out of large wooden buckets. Each trapa removes his own bowl from his vest in order to receive his portion. The bowls bear the pattern of the particular sect and must be used by even the highest dignitaries, as no china or silver is permitted at such meetings. Wealthy monasteries allow for thickly buttered tea, enough for the monks to blow off and collect in small pots to sell or fill their personal lamps with. Altar lamps must be replenished with a new stock of butter each

time, so that there is often enough butter to go round for a poor trapa's personal use. Families usually send *tsampa* (barley flour), which the monk might mix with his tea. Sometimes the monastery kitchen serves tsampa and a piece of butter along with the tea, or soup instead of tea. And sometimes—presumably after a large donation from a rich merchant—the meal will feature both tea *and* soup. Money is distributed to the monks during mealtimes.

Hermits begin their training as trapas in these gompas. When they have achieved their contemplative goals, they wander into the mountain fastness and spend the remainder of their lives meditating in lonely hermitages. Male children are brought to monasteries at age eight. Here, under the eyes of a tutor who remains his teacher throughout the entire course, the boy (if he is wealthy) will flourish, learn, and provide his superiors with butter, meat, and plenty of tsampa. High-class children get the most noteworthy and desirable teachers. Low-class boys (*geyogs*) must do menial labor and act as servants in order to obtain their education. Novices all share in the profits of the gompa at large, as well as in its occasional gifts and endowments from wealthy devotees.

Lamaseries (monastic colleges) provide the next stage of training. Boys from unconnected gompas would leave at the end of their tenure and study at one of the four large Tibetan colleges. Here, a serious student might learn philoso-

Hopefully, these young boys will have enough food sent from home to provide them with the best tutors. If they come from poor families, they must work their way through the training, which may last twelve years or more.

phy and metaphysics at the *Tsen nid* department, and ritual and magic in the *Gyud* department. Chinese and Indian medicine were taught in the *Men* division, while sacred scriptures were in the province of the *Do* college. Grammar, science, and math were taught by private tutors not in connection with the university.

The situation is greatly changed since the Tibetans have been exiled from their country by the Chinese, who have destroyed the Buddhist monasteries and now forbid monastic training of any sort. The remnants of the Tibetan community reside under the Dalai Lama's rulership in Darjeeling, northern India.

In the days before the Chinese invasion, the philosophy department sponsored exciting debates, in the lamasery's open courtyards, which formed a highlight of the school term. The event was as ritualistic as it was intellectual—with young men turning their rosaries around their arms to certain prescribed patterns, clapping and stamping as they asked their questions, and jumping about while answering their opponents. The winner was always carried aloft on the shoulders of his vanquished rival.

In the college of magic, students spent their time learning the methods of dealing with evil spirits. There, young monks allotted a certain period for worshiping the leftover gods of their Bön ancestors in order to tame them.

Monks of the Red Cap sect permitted marriage, while Yellow Caps remained celibate. Wives were not permitted to live on gompa grounds with their husbands when the men retired there for meditation and festivals. (Many a lama escaped a touchy situation with this excuse.) During these rituals the entire group would meet in the assembly for scriptural reading and announcements from the hierarchy.

Should a monk require a special service for his own personal needs, he would ask a colleague to perform the necessary rites. Yet, in his spiritual development, only he could work for and by himself—through intense meditation or, for followers of the Short Path, through magic.

So there appeared to be three acceptable methods for divine realization in Tibetan yoga: orthodox Buddhist ritual and prayer, meditation, and magic. Only his teacher could intrude on a monk's chosen method; yet, although there was no need for him to attend regular religious services, the trapa would occasionally light some incense in prayer for a special favor, or he might bow to a statue of the Buddha.

Novices lived in separate apartments, each according to his means. Unlike Indian monks who believed in austerity and renunciation of worldly living, the Tibetans often supplied themselves ostentatiously. Each monk would redo the apartment he had inherited or bought from its former tenant. Poor monks rented rooms in the houses of wealthier ones. Students, or old novices, lived free in the homes of rich lamas. Those lucky enough to serve a tulku often became rich and famous themselves. Artistic or especially gifted trapas sustained themselves by practicing their arts. Doctors, shopkeepers, astrologers, and painters earned a comfortable income from their trades.

Fund raising on a large scale took place twice or three times a year. Donations were obtained by begging, working, or trading. Money and other personal effects were put aside by treasurer monks whose responsibility it was to provide butter, food, and building repairs for the monastery at large. The system resembled an escrow account which, after a certain period, must be repaid with interest. If the treasurer monk was clever, he might have doubled the original amount, and could therefore keep what was left after repayment of the balance and interest. Some monasteries were powerful landlords, owning large estates and entire populations over which they ruled. These estates required entire governments, including police, mayors, town councils, and so forth. Officials were dressed regally in ceremonial clothing covered with jewels. Policemen monks (*dobdobs*) were recruited from the lower classes and took special delight in making themselves feared by smearing grease over their faces and wearing dirty rags.

Only the tulkus took no part in the ordinary life of the monastery. This aristocratic caste was founded by the Gelugpa sect's fifth Grand Lama in A.D. 1650. Lobzang Gyatso arbitrarily decided one day that he was an incarnation of the Bodhisattva Chenrezigs (the Indian Buddha of Compassion). From that time on, it was open season on tulkus, with monasteries everywhere creating their own whenever they felt like it. Most of these are incarnations of saints, gods, or heroes. Sometimes they even remember their past lives and predict at their deaths exactly where and when and to whom they will be reborn. Powerful tulkus are so spiritually developed that they can manifest themselves in many worlds at once in the form of many different incarnations. Like the advanced Indian *sannyasi*, they are supposedly capable of moving mountains, bringing storms, and foreseeing the future.

With special training, the tulku, and only the tulku, may guide the soul of a dead person from its corpse. Uttering

A Tibetan lamasery, where—before the Chinese invasion—young men studied mathematics and magic at the same time.

hik and *phat* in a rhythmic cadence that eventually makes a straw stand upright at the top of the dead man's head, the tulku (who has made a small hole in the skull) ushers the soul out. If he is managing the performance in the absence of a corpse, he must be very careful not to say the words hik and phat in such a way that it will kill *him*. Since Tibetan yogis are believed to maintain their consciousness after dying, it is only necessary for the tulku to assist ordinary souls on their way, leaving yogis to manage for themselves. Identi-

fying with the dying man, the practitioner must instruct him, filling him in on the details of what he should expect to find on the next plane of existence. To make it work, the tulku must spend a specified period in the presence of the corpse, even eating and drinking in its company.

Tibetans believe in maintaining consciousness after death so that a person may select his next birth willingly rather than be flung into any family at random. It is a great blessing to be born into a family of yogis, for example. So it is important that the newly departed soul be aware of what is happening to it on the other side. Many vivid and sometimes terrifying experiences await the soul in *bardo* (purgatory). You can therefore imagine how essential it is for the ordinary person to have an experienced yogi lead him through all the hells and heavens he is supposed to find after dying.

Our own version of this situation is the relationship between the psychiatrist and his patient. The doctor leads the frightened person through the maze of his consciousness to a kind of mental "rebirth."

The priest listening to the dying patient unburden himself of his fears, guilt, fantasies, represents another aspect of the same journey.

Two years after the tulku has died, astrologers (only those who are themselves verified tulkus) are called in to assist in finding the reborn saint. Through tracing various obscure signs and interpreting equally difficult language, the child is eventually found. Sometimes it takes as long as ten years to discover his whereabouts, and sometimes—to the great sorrow of the monastery involved in the search—he is never found at all. The tulku's rich and luxurious life is an enviable one, so it is no surprise that many families are eager to have their children selected. Any child suspected of being the reborn tulku is carefully studied by a clairvoyant lama, whose favorable pronouncement brings about the following test:

A grouping of religious objects like rosaries, books, teacups and ritual implements is presented to the child, who is told to pick something. If he picks the object belonging to the dead tulku, he is a good candidate. If more than one child makes the right choice, or if a number of clairvoyant lamas disagree, further tests are devised. Once the right child is chosen, however, his parents are moved into the monastery until he no longer requires his mother's care. When they are moved, the boy's mother and father take up lodging in a comfortable house owned by the monastery, where they are provided with all they need for the rest of their days.

Being a tulku makes one automatically enlightened at birth, with everything built in, as it were. But achieving Buddhahood in one lifetime, without the benefits of former incarnations, is a very different story. If we remember that giving up the world is at the heart of all Oriental religious philosophy, that even the body itself must become unreal to the seeker, then we can better understand what would otherwise strike us as morbid or simply suicidal.

The young lama being trained according to the rules of the Short Path (magic) must become well acquainted with startling situations that will evoke inner reflection. Some novices are tied out in the open to a rock and left there alone to challenge whatever demons they manage to call down. Hallucinations are not hard to come by when you are tied for three days and nights, sleepless, hungry, and desperate for any activity at all. The weaker students are often eliminated forever.

The terrifying ritual called *chöd* easily separates the potential superman from the ordinary run of mortal. The monk is thrust into a desolate, frightening place in pitch darkness. Territory where awful things have happened is most to be preferred. Following a prescribed script which includes his dancing and jumping about wildly while reciting prayers, the trapa must accompany himself with the proper bells, drums, and a trumpet made of human thighbone. It's a wonder he can move around at all, bearing so much equipment. The entire ritual is gruesomely symbolic of the death of the devotee's worldly desires. To this end, he celebrates a Red Meal and a Black Meal, during which he sees himself being devoured by demons. If he is too affected by the process, he risks illness, madness, or actual death. One monastery, founded more than two hundred years ago, featured chöd as its leading trial. Solitary houses (*tsams khang*) where no communication was permitted formed the living quarters of the monks in this sect. For men who have succeeded in the terrible ritual, it is no longer necessary to go out and perform. Merely meditating on the experience brings on the power gained through the supreme renunciation of the self. A group of older monks may occasionally get together and perform chöd to mark the anniversary of their first experiences with it. But in groups, the chöd celebrants are more inclined to feast and take pleasure in the recollection of a job well done. Here is a detailed description of a chöd performance.

The young man is left alone in a burial ground at night. After calling down all the demons he can remember, he begins to dance on one foot with stomping and leaping movements while making music of his prayers. Then he reaches for his bell, *dorje* (thunderbolt), and magic dagger (phurba).

After performing the proper ritual gestures, he plays his instruments as he sings of the destruction of all selfishness, passion, and desire. Blowing on his human thighbone trumpet, he calls down the hungry demons, asking them to feast on his body. Picturing the goddess who represents his own ego, he continues calling until the figure has taken on a strange life of its own and come down to face him with a sword in her hand. The goddess suddenly strikes out and cuts off the novice's head, then his arms and legs, and then she slits open his belly, disemboweling him. Calling all the demons to join her, she begins a terrible banquet, noisily chewing on every part of the poor devotee's dismembered body. He, all the while, is urging on the diners with his chanting:

> *For ages, in the course of renewed births, I have borrowed from countless living beings—at the cost of their welfare and life—food, clothing, all kinds of services to sustain my body, to keep it joyful in comfort and to defend it against death. Today I pay my debt, offering for destruction this body which I have held so dear . . .*

> *I give my flesh to the hungry, my blood to the thirsty, my skin to clothe those who are naked, my bones as fuel to those who suffer from cold. I give my happiness to the unhappy ones. I give my breath to bring back the dying to life. . . .*

> *Shame on me if I shrink from giving my self! Shame on you, wretched and demoniac beings, if you do not dare to prey upon it. . . .*

And so he concludes the Red Meal portion of his ordeal. If he still has the strength, he now embarks upon the Black Meal ritual. The vision vanishes and he is once again alone in the windswept burial yard. Now he begins to see himself as nothing more than a pile of charred bones sticking out of a stream of black mud which represents all the miserable and evil deeds he has committed during the course of repeated lifetimes. Building himself up to a sacrificial pitch, he realizes that even the idea of destroying himself is illusory, that he has nothing at all to give away, indeed, not even a "self," since he *is* nothing. Because his very sense of identity is an illusion, he has nothing to renounce. And now, with this new realization of selflessness, the ascetic ends the chöd.

These very real visions occur while the celebrant is in a trance state during which he still remains aware of his surroundings. Tibetan yogis (like their Indian counterparts) make a point of seeking isolated, quiet places as a setting for their meditations. This is important to a man who has broken all material ties and distractions and therefore cannot speak to someone who might interrupt or threaten him. Should he come very quickly out of his contemplations, the yogi may experience discomfort and even pain. Thus, there are special rules for "coming out," as it were: turning the head slowly from side to side, massaging the forehead and crown, stretching the arms and clasping hands while bending the body backwards. These and other hints are given to the practitioner by his *tsawai* lama, if he is lucky enough to have connected up with his spiritual teacher of past lives. Second choice for a guide would be a fond relative or loyal friend. Ties formed between such teachers and pupils are believed to result from good "past deeds."

Advanced students are taught to control the body by learning spectacular feats like levitation. The tsawai lama, though he may spend a long time teaching his trapa such supernormal controls, is always quick to remind him that he must regard it as an exercise in will and nothing more. The student must begin by sitting cross-legged on a cushion. Inhaling slowly, he gradually allows his breathing to grow shallow until he holds his breath back altogether. With air held in his lungs, he leaps up, still cross-legged, and without

Lamas who wish to perform the chöd *ritual must conjure up demons as terrifying as those pictured here.*

using his hands—if possible. Then he falls back onto the cushion in the same posture. This exercise, when repeated many times, is said to facilitate extraordinarily high leaps. The body supposedly grows so light and weightless that yogis who have perfected the art can sit on a stalk of barley without crushing, or even bending it.

When the student feels ready to test his levitating ability, he digs a pit in the ground equal in depth to his own height. Then he builds a dome over the pit, leaving a small opening at the top. The distance between the cross-legged yogi seated at the base of the pit is now twice the length of his body. If he can jump cross-legged through the small hole at the top of the dome, he has passed the test. Spiritual assistance or, as Tibetans believe, direct transmission of power from the disciple's teacher, is called *angkur*. This kind of grace often plays a part in assisting the yogi more quickly than his own exertions might allow.

Now, "levitating" means different things to different people. Through certain breathing techniques which increase the oxygen supply to the brain, we can give ourselves the feeling that we are "lightheaded" or "high." With yogic training, novices probably induce the sensation of floating rather than sitting solidly on the ground. Whether they physically levitate a few inches from the ground or not has yet to be proven.

Many of the Tibetan practices are subjective experiences designed to prove to the candidate that *all* experience (both sitting *and* levitating) are merely passing states of mind.

Flaming gods with fierce looks are the order of the day for the lama interested in obtaining supernormal powers.

Such is also the case with the tumo exercise mentioned before. The ability to generate body heat to a supernormal degree requires long and arduous training. Since it has been rather definitively outlined by Tibetan masters, let us examine the procedure in detail:

First the student must wear nothing but a simple cotton loincloth. Really brave disciples wear nothing. Novices start by sitting outdoors on a straw mat; more advanced students sit on the snow or even on top of an ice mound. No food or drink, especially nothing hot, is permitted before practicing. The man may sit in the lotus posture or with both legs on the ground, if he prefers using a stool. The *mudra* (symbolic hand gesture) consists of an extended forefinger and pinky, with the middle and fourth fingers folded into the palm. Again the yogi practices rhythmic breathing, holding breath and, in exhaling, imagining that all anger, lust, selfishness, etc. are being tossed out of the system. At the other end, with each inhalation, he imagines that all Buddha qualities —love, compassion, purity of heart—are flowing into him.

With a peaceful mind, he visualizes a golden lotus flower at his navel. Within the shining flower, he imagines the syllable *ram*. Above this he sees the syllable *ma* (Rama being an incarnation of God), from which a female deity, Dorgee Naljorma, emerges. Every letter of these syllables must be regarded by the yogi as a living and powerful entity filled with fire. Now he continues the process by identifying himself with the goddess and placing the letter *a* in the navel and the syllable *ha* at the crown of his head. The breathing now becomes like a bellows fanning up a low flame that assumes the shape of a ball within the letter *a*. With each breath taken, the force of the flames seated in the navel grows stronger. Holding the breath for longer and longer periods, the yogi concentrates hard on the increasing fire as it moves upward from the navel through the *uma* vein. The uma is visualized first as a thin thread filled with flame and currents of breath. Then it grows, expanding from a finger's width to an arm's width, and at last filling the entire body with a blaze of flame and air. The man now loses all bodily consciousness, seeing himself as nothing more than a flaming vein in a sea of fire. It takes at least an hour to reach this stage.

Working backward now, the yogi reverses the steps of his visions, as his mind drops all sense of observation and merges with the Void. In this trance he no longer has any sense of cold, no sense of being either perceived or perceiver. Suspended beyond the senses, the yogi may now remain in meditative bliss (samadhi) for as long as he wishes. Experienced practitioners of tumo claim that a pleasant level of heat is sustained by the body throughout.

Young potential tumo experts are brought by their lama guides to frozen shores on cold and windy winter nights. The disciples are then seated naked and cross-legged on the ice while sheets dipped in icy water are wrapped around them. When the sheets are dried immediately by a man's body heat, the lamas are convinced of his success. The yogi who dries the most sheets is declared winner of this bizarre competition, and is thereafter known as a *respa*—he who wears a cotton loincloth during all seasons and in all climes.

Our version of these wonders is called hypnosis. Here, even ordinary people, when put into altered mental states, have felt no pain when needles were stuck through their arms, and no cold even in severest winter weather. We have only begun to study these "altered states of consciousness" in the West. Perhaps the Tibetans, in their own experiments,

have gone farther. After all, they have a few centuries' head start.

An even more explicit example of the trainee's dependence on his master's angkur is telepathy training. First the student learns to concentrate his mind on a single thought or symbol to the exclusion of all else. Then he must become proficient at analyzing his own moods, reactions, physical symptoms, and memories (like a free-associating patient, who must at the same time be his own psychoanalyst). After he has practiced alone for a while, the student works together with his lama. Seated together in a quiet, dark place, they concentrate on the same object. When they break for intermission, they discuss the disciple's thought pattern and compare it with the teacher's own, noting the likenesses and differences along the way. Resuming meditation, the student now empties his mind and watches his thoughts as if they belonged to someone outside himself. Noting all images and speculations, he again compares them with what the lama has been mentally suggesting to him.

In the next phase, pupil and teacher work at a distance, the former acting on what he believes are the suggestions given him by his master. If he is right, the discipline continues at a further distance. In between sessions with his lama, a student may experiment with a friend by sending him messages when he least expects them and comparing notes afterward. Really adept yogis may send messages even to people they don't know, and some work with animals (like thinking: "Come here, Spot" to their dogs). Some study

The mandala is an occult symbol used by monks for meditation, and magicians for evocation.

telepathy for years with no results. Unlike levitating or dry-ing sheets with your body heat, telepathy seems, for the most part, to be an inborn talent.

Once the student has undergone his probationary trials and errors, the lama conducts him across more metaphysical ground. He might draw and explain symbolic diagrams (*mandalas*) and teach him how to meditate on their inner meaning; or he will explain the nature of *tawa* (looking and examining), *gompa* (thinking and meditating), *Chyöd pa* (practicing and realizing).

Again, all of these techniques lead to the same goal: con-centration of the mind to a point where it is emptied of all thought. The mandala, a circular drawing embellished by geometric designs, helps the yogi to focus on a visual image with all his might. You may have experienced this kind of concentration, which eliminates all other thoughts or distrac-tions: while playing an instrument, working hard on a mathe-matics problem, or writing a poem.

Even philosophizing is seen as a legitimate route to per-fect wisdom. "Looking and examining," for the yogi, is the method used by intellectual-type thinkers. One might study a cow—the physical object, the nature of "cowness," the idea in our minds when the word appears without the actual cow standing before us. When we go beyond reason and identify ourselves (observer) with the object of our observa-tions—that is, become one with "cow"—then we have real-ized the true nature of the mind.

Take the following story as a perfect example of Oriental idealism:

A student was told to clear his mind and concentrate on nothing. When his guru approached him after a while, the student complained: "I empty my mind and then find my-self thinking of my pet bull."

"Very well," said the guru, "concentrate entirely on your pet bull."

For a few days he left the student to his meditations. When he returned, he called toward the window of the hut, asking his student to come out.

"I can't," cried the student. "My horns are too wide for this door."

The guru knew then that his pupil was on his way to enlightenment, and again departed.

To reinforce his lessons, the lama advises the pupil to retire into isolation for a while. This is called going into tsams, remaining in one's quarters for a fixed period during which one prays, contemplates, and does a little bit of work. Some pupils are permitted one or two guests every so often, others go so far as to shade the windows and lock the doors, receiving their food through a specially created flap. Certain monasteries provide tsams khang, small houses specifically geared for this purpose. Particularly dedicated yogis have been known to remain in tsams for years. And there are even those who live out their entire lives in this form of meditative isolation. A permanent hermit's dwelling is a hut or cave known as a *ritöd*.

What are these yogis doing when they "meditate"? As the focal point of all training, Buddhist meditation consists of eliminating all thought from the mind so that the student may reach a point beyond mind that can only be described as super—or transcendental—consciousness: a wordless, formless state that provides the practitioner with peace, tranquility, and bliss. Preparation for the Tibetan variety of meditation is called *niampar jagpa*, stilling the movement of the mind. Try sitting quietly without thinking, and you'll see just how difficult this is. By calming down the chain reactive flow of thoughts, yogis achieve new psychic conditions that eliminate all former ideas about self, ego, identification with the body.

In the highest reaches beyond mind, the Tibetans believe, lies the truth about the unity of all created beings. Here in the Great Void lies the secret: that all beasts, humans, devils, gods, and planets are no more than mirages scattered across the eternally playing mind of God. Thus the imperfect human mind must be purified throughout a lifetime of mental and physical discipline which surpasses in its importance all other material needs: home, family, riches, fame . . . everything we consider worth living for in our world. Should he fail, the powerful force within the yogi's being will never vibrate, but rather remain asleep for many lifetimes more—along with the rest of us. The great opportunity for the yogi, therefore, is always *now*, this very minute. The ignorant will remain sunk in their ignorant sleep for centuries, but that is not his business. He must be on his way. He must rouse himself from the dream in search of his own innermost truth.

Those who attain this form of psychic perfection are few; those who have attained it in one lifetime are none but the Buddha himself. When a monk feels he is ready to give up all in search of perfect wisdom, he asks to be released from his religious orders as a hermit or a wanderer. His revered lama will most likely warn him that such a move is madness, that he will no doubt return a broken shadow of himself. When, still determined to go, he fights against all argument, the seeker has two stones removed from the ring given him by his lama, the missing stones reminding him of his separation and loss. After many years, if the monk returns, the stones are replaced and remain in the ring, which, from that point until his death, is never removed. Should he succeed in his search for perfection, he will be embalmed at death rather than cremated—with the ring on display near his body.

All who look upon his remains, and especially at the ring, now kneel in reverence to his greatness. He has achieved the title of Grand Lama. Tibetans believe that the spirits of such men live on after them, and that there is a secret world-wide priesthood comprised of great masters who, with their powerful and elevated angkur, transmit grace and spiritual assistance to us all.

At the other end of the spectrum lies the magician. Where the yogi seeks to strip himself of all possessions, powers—mental and physical—and emerges desireless and serene, the ngagspas are riddled with cravings for control over everything, from the elements to the demons inhabiting every planet, and then some. In short, the magician wants to control everything but himself. Note that where the yogi lives with a minimum of possessions, the sorcerer is loaded down with objects: symbolic charts and figurines, horns, plants, ritual formulas, daggers, and the like. A simple implement—the horn used for stopping hailstorms, say—must be intricately carved. Inside there must be tiny pieces of metal and mustard seed. It must be black and white, with a carved tortoise in the center. The body of the tortoise must bear a circle divided into nine portions on each of which the following Tibetan numbers are inscribed:

Top: 4 9 2
Middle: 3 5 7
Bottom: 8 1 6

On either side of the tortoise there is a scorpion; between each of these lies a temple-shaped building known as a *chorten.* The top of the horn takes the shape of a coiled serpent whose opening is covered with a brass lid engraved with a cross formed of two dorjes, ritual thunderbolts. Without the metal dorje in his hand, the sorcerer is impotent. As if he didn't have enough to worry about, he must himself supply the inside of the horn with rye or mustard seed, pounded metals like gold and silver, copper, or iron. And even then, in order to halt his hailstorm effectively, he must prepare himself three days in advance by reciting Sanskrit prayers that can only be uttered after fasting and meditation! At last, breathing into the horn at the narrow end, he prays out in the field as he sprinkles the mustard seeds in the direction of the storm. Theoretically, even the biggest droplets of hail will be shattered by his shouts before they have a chance to fall.

The more intellectual type of diviner, the *jyotishi*, will take a few deep breaths and answer any question you put to him. He may distract you with some mystical signs drawn on paper, or he may check into a book whose pages are covered with pictures of animals or flowers. When you put your finger on one of the images, he recites the names of the stars or chants a mantra (mystical sounds). Most often he will answer your question correctly. The jyotishi is a natural for television.

Morbid magicians, in search of power from a highly psychic human being who has recently died, will go to extreme lengths to dine on a piece of the corpse's flesh. Such a banquet is said to produce supernatural powers in the diner. Others get assurances of their power from making corpses get up and dance. This has made certain Tibetan magicians very famous, and their techniques are known far and wide. Here is how it goes:

The sorcerer, locked up in a dark room with a corpse, lies down on it and performs mouth-to-mouth resuscitation, all

This young wandering lama is equipped for his travels with a rosary, charm box, human thighbone trumpet, and small drum.

the while repeating a magic formula and thinking of nothing else. When the corpse begins to stand up and move around, the magician clings fast and doesn't let it escape, no matter how hard the dead man tries to get away. This might involve some wild escapades in which both magician and corpse are leaping around face to face with lips pressed together. Suddenly—and this is the big moment—the tongue pops out of the dead man's mouth. Taking the tongue in his own mouth, and biting it off, the sorcerer at once lets go of the body, which falls down in a heap. Should he let go or lose his grip on the dead man after having revived him, the ngagspa is a dead man himself. Why, you may ask, would anyone

want to indulge in such a dance macabre? The answer—to the sorcerer—is a simple one: Carefully dried corpse-tongues bear exceptionally potent magical qualities.

The indispensable ritual weapon known as the phurba is a dagger made of bronze, wood, or ivory with elaborate carvings on it. The magician supposedly invests it with his own powerful vibrations, thus charging the phurba with a frightful energy all its own. Finally, after many years, the weapon grows possessed and must not be kept in the house where any layman might get hold of it. This kind of psychic energy resides in centers of the body called *khorlos*, which are found in all of us. Seen as lotus-shaped, they are specifically located at the base of the spine, at the navel, at the solar plexus, at the heart, throat, between the eyebrows, and at the crown of the head. Most of us don't know they are there and therefore make no use of them. The magician usually limits his activities to the lower khorlos. The aim of the yogi, on the other hand, is to bring the energy from the lowest point at the base of the spine to the *dabtong* (thousand-petaled lotus) at the crown of the head in a direct stream of divine light.

This being an almost superhuman task, the magician too often rests content with concentrating his thoughts on auxiliary mind forms which he "creates" in order to carry out his bidding. After years of reciting certain formulas at ritual images he has himself made out of rags or clay, the sorcerer will confront one of these *yidam* in person. He knows this when he can feel the touch of its hand, or speak to it, or watch it walk around in his cell. The only problem is that

The primitive Bön faith is combined with Buddhism by monks like these who still worship the old bloodthirsty gods.

this thought form may in the end assume too much real strength and drive the magician crazy.

Many of us have had "imaginary friends" in our childhood. These inventions helped us get through hard times; creatures like Jiminy Cricket and Tinkerbell and Ali Baba's genie represent a child's need to master the grown-up world. Perhaps the yidam is meant to represent a similar psychological state for Tibetans—along with the warning that too much fantasy can be harmful indeed.

Healer magicians use their energy (*tsal* or *shugs*) to charge pills, holy water, and talismans. Before doing so, however, they too must purify themselves with the proper diet, bath, and meditation. This process can take weeks or months; one wonders what has happened to the patient in the meantime.

Those Tibetan sorcerers who claim invisibility as one of their numerous powers state that they accomplish this by ceasing all mental activity. By withdrawing themselves so completely from the attention of other people that they arouse no reflective images in their minds and leave no mark on their memories, the magicians attain "invisibility." Out of mind, out of sight, so to speak.

Most of these practices come from the old Bön beliefs that predate the civilizing influence of Buddhism. Yet, like all "primitive" peoples who have acquired their religion from missionaries, the Tibetans managed to have their cake and eat it too. Using Buddhist prayers like *Om Mani Padme Hum* (the jewel at the heart of the lotus) and reciting it backward, the Bön-trained magician may kill, heal, grow or wither crops, or foretell the future. Brandishing the inevitable bones, hair, and teeth that make up the stock in trade of magicians all over the world, they gather in lonely clearings with their disciples. The tribute to Buddhism may be found in the bowl of burning incense, but the old blood sacrifice hasn't been entirely done away with. The offering may be meat from a freshly killed yak, or skin to appease the spirit.

The chief sorcerer blows three short blasts on his magic horn to the background cry of the crowd, which now invokes the terrible god of death: *"Yamantaka!"* Three times the cry rends the night air, while the faithful all concentrate as one on the image of the monstrous god of the Bön, a bull with fangs, horns, and a pig's snout whose lips drip blood and whose enormous hooves are stamping on human bodies, its apron of skulls glowing in light cast by the twisted flames of hell. When the spirit appears and accepts the food sacrifice, the master magician asks him for favors. Any one of the worshipers whose attention flags for even a second runs the risk of permanent blindness or disease.

Some sorcerers walk on fire to propitiate the spirit of fire. Others meditate on demons in order to acquire advice from them. All agree, however, that talismans and symbolic devices are all merely the external trappings of magic, that—in the end—the *true* powers live within the mind of the magician himself.

(Overleaf) Milarepa the magician, poet, and hermit.

Jetsun Milarepa

The great "cotton clad" saint of Tibet, Milarepa, was born on August 25, 1051, in Kyanga, in the Tsa province of Gungthang on the frontier with Nepal. His wealthy parents named him Tho-pa-ga, "Delightful to hear," and showered him with comforts throughout his childhood. Then, when the boy was seven, his father died, changing all the early joy to hardship and leaving the family to the treachery of his relatives. Milarepa's uncle and aunt, as guardians of the estate, subjected the widow and her children to harsh labor and eventually succeeded in cheating them out of their inheritance altogether. To avenge her miserable plight, the boy's mother determined to send him to a black magic school in order that he might curse her relatives and ease the family's condition. When still a youngster, Milarepa was therefore sent to a tantric guru who taught him the art of evoking hailstorms.

Too successful at his magic, the young man returned home and literally *brought the house down* around his relatives, many of whom were killed outright. Milarepa's mother leaped around in the streets, not hesitating to exhibit her spiteful pleasure to all who passed. The relatives of those who had died in the catastrophe grew enraged and vowed to fight back. Thus a lifelong feud was begun. Still unsatisfied, Milarepa's vengeful mother pleaded with him to make a colossal hailstorm that would kill her brother-in-law's entire barley crop for the season. Though torn between conscience for what he had already done and love for his mother, Milarepa conjured a terrible storm which ruined every bit of his uncle's crop that year.

Both Milarepa and his guru felt guilty, however, and agreed to work off their bad deeds by turning to the right-hand path and away from black magic forever. Directed by a lama to Marpa the Translator, a famed scholar with supernatural powers, Milarepa experienced his first real pang of faith. "I was walking along the road, when I came upon a heavily built lama, rather inclined to corpulence, with full eyes, but very dignified in appearance. He was plowing. The moment my eyes fell upon him, I was thrilled by a feeling of inexpressibly ecstatic bliss, in which I lost all consciousness of my surroundings."

Subjecting him to a continued series of tests and trials, Marpa feigned short temper, severe looks, ill will, and spite toward his new student in order to erase the diabolical effects of the black magic he had indulged in before turning religious. Like the Zen monastic practice of keeping the begging disciple in the outer courtyard for three days, the Tibetan lama's discipline is designed to build the aspirant up to a peak of faith and patience. Only after such ordeals can he determine the level of the student's capacity.

Milarepa, from early on, showed a saint's patience. Each day, at Marpa's orders, he went out and worked on a house for the guru's eldest son. And each day Marpa came out in a rage and made him tear it down again. Milarepa developed huge sores on his back from all the hard labor, but he said nothing. Whenever he tried to join the disciples' circle to obtain initiation, however, Marpa demanded some payment. Then, angrily rejecting Milarepa's offer, he would push him out of the circle, kicking and insulting him in the bargain.

One day Marpa's wife, a kind-hearted woman who had taken a liking to the young and badly treated student, interceded in his behalf with her husband. Marpa sent for his disciple and asked him to show his back. Milarepa now felt some hope—but not for long. Marpa looked at the sores and said: "This is nothing to the trials and tribulations which were endured by my Lord Saint Naropa [Marpa's own guru]. He had to undergo in his own body twelve greater and twelve lesser trials, making twenty-four in all. I myself did not spare my wealth or consider my body's safety, but, sacrificing both ungrudgingly, followed and served my teacher Naropa. If thou art really in search of the Truth, do not boast so about thy services, but continue waiting patiently and working steadily till thy building task is entirely finished." Then he advised Milarepa to roll his coat into a pad and wear it on his back as donkeys do!

Months went by in this fashion until, with the help of Marpa's wife, Milarepa invented a little scheme in the hope of getting Marpa to relent and initiate him. Pretending to be leaving in sorrow, while Mrs. Marpa begged him loudly to remain, Milarepa succeeded only in drawing from his teacher a harder beating than ever. At this point, humiliated both in body and in ego, he made his way to the home of another

guru, one who had been Marpa's own disciple in the past.
Here, under false circumstances, he was initiated. But because he had come to the new guru without gaining Marpa's
permission, he made no progress whatever in his meditations.

At last, after confessing to his new guru that he had come
to him under false pretenses, he made a return trip. Apolo-
gizing for his rashness, Milarepa finds that Marpa is now
ready to take him into the fold. In the company of all his disciples, Marpa declares the real reasons for his cruel treatment
of Milarepa:

> *Should there be any one amongst you who are
> seated here who, not understanding the religious
> motive, feels shocked at these things, I exhort him
> not to be shaken in his faith and belief. Had I had
> the chance of plunging this spiritual son of mine
> nine times into utter despair, he would have been
> cleansed thoroughly of all his sins. He would have
> disappeared totally, his physical body being forever
> dissolved; he would have attained nirvana. That it
> will not be so, and that he will still retain a small
> portion of his demerits is due to [my wife's] ill-timed
> pity and narrow understanding. However, he hath
> been subjected to eight deep tribulations, which
> have cleansed him of the heavier sins; and he hath
> suffered many minor chastenings, which will purify
> him from minor sins. Now I am going to care for
> him and give him those teachings and initiations
> which I hold as dear as my own heart. I myself will
> provide him with food while he is in retreat, and
> with my own hands will enclose him in the place of
> meditation. Henceforth rejoice.*

That night Milarepa is shaven and pronounced a monk. As Marpa blesses the wine during the religious rites, the entire company sees a rainbowlike halo around the cup; the tutelary gods appear, announcing the initiation of a great saint.

For eleven months Milarepa sat in isolated contemplation in a nearby cave. Meditating each day with a lighted lamp on his head, he remained motionless until the light went out. Food was brought at the end of the period, comprising the length of a religious festival; until then he had no idea whether it was night or morning, winter or summer. As a result of his meditations, Milarepa successfully realized his divine nature and eliminated all sense of ego. Like Hakuin and all the other "realized" masters, Milarepa describes this condition as *superconsciousness*. He regards the forms that appear during meditation as worthless and advocates "a keen power of analysis . . . inquisitive intellect" and the capacity for prolonged *shi-nay*, mental quiet. "The very first effort must be made in a compassionate mood, with the aim of dedicating the merit of one's efforts to the Universal Good. Secondly, the goal of one's aspirations must be well defined and clear, soaring into the regions transcending thought. Finally, there is need of mentally praying and wishing for blessings on others so earnestly that one's mind processes also transcend thought . . . One must sacrifice bodily ease and all luxuriousness, and, with this in mind, face and surmount every obstacle, being ever willing to sacrifice life itself, and prepared for every possible contingency." After a brief period in the company of his guru, Milarepa retreated once again and remained in secluded meditation for several more years in a cave near Marpa's home.

One day he suddenly finds himself homesick and worried about his mother. When he begs Marpa's permission to go home, his guru tells him that they will not meet again on earth, and gives him further secret religious instruction before they part. Designating Milarepa as his spiritual heir, and therefore chief of the *Kargyupta* sect founded by Naropa, Marpa warns him: "The method adopted by Tilopa in disciplining Naropa, and by me in converting thee, will not be very suitable for degenerate beings of the future, who will be narrow of heart, and incapable of understanding the sublimest of the Truths. Therefore, beware of adopting that method of instruction." (It is well known among Tibetans that Milarepa, unlike his own guru, thereafter became the mildest, most compassionate of teachers.)

Sending him off, Marpa advises Milarepa of his ascetic nature and advocates that he spend his life away from the world. "Spend your time in caves and on mountain tops," he says, giving him a magic scroll that will save him from a foreseen danger later on. Amid much weeping, guru and loyal disciple are parted. By supernatural methods (*Lum go pa*, exceptionally fast walking that resembles jogging along on a pogo stick) Milarepa makes the three- or four-month journey home in only three days.

But when he arrives, he finds his house in ruins, his sister gone, and his mother dead. Reacting with despair and disgust over his past attachments to the world, Milarepa vows to cut himself off from it.

"Henceforth, the world had nothing to tempt me or to bind me to it. I repeated my vows to devote my life to a rigid course of asceticism in the realization of the Truth, and resolved to adhere to them firmly."

Once again he meets his evil aunt, only this time, instead of cursing her, Milarepa responds to her taunts by giving up to her his house and field. Now he is penniless, without even his inherited estate, nothing at all to live on. As a gift of conscience, the aunt supplies him with some food for his seclusion, and Milarepa departs for the Dragkar-Taso cave with the resolution not to descend to any village or town.

Here he commences a period of extreme mortification in the hope of attaining full enlightenment. Without thought of body, Milarepa lives for years on nettle broth alone. Naked, he finds his body shrinking and turning as green as the nettles he eats, and covered with a blanket of greenish hair. In between meditations, he looks at his guru's scroll, touches his head with it in order to build up his courage. The scroll, he finds, has the ability to appease his hunger when he merely touches his stomach with it. Sometimes it even makes him feel full, and he burps! There are times when he is tempted to open it and read what lies inside, but something always holds him back. The time, he knows, has not yet arrived.

One day his long-lost sister, who has heard about him from travelers, appears at the opening of Milarepa's cave. Seeing her brother a living corpse, she weeps and pleads with him to at least go out and beg for food. After she has finished feeding him with some wholesome nourishment, Milarepa finds that he is ill, that he can't digest the good food and will die. Now he opens the scroll and finds in it instructions to give up his nettle diet for a wholesome one, to develop a stronger bodily constitution which will enable him to undergo even deeper stages of meditation. The sister departs, her pleas having come to nothing.

But now Milarepa learns that, by living through the experience of a kind of "death in life," he has so *dematerialized* his body that he can transform himself into any shape and can even fly on occasion.

By day, I thus felt that I could exercise endless phenomenal powers; by night, in my dreams, I could traverse the universe in every direction unimpededly . . . and I saw everything clearly [as I went]. Likewise [in my dreams] I could multiply myself into hundreds of personalities, all endued with the same powers as myself. . . . I could also transform my physical body into a blazing mass of fire, or into an expanse of flowing or calm water.

As his reputation grew, Milarepa found it necessary to move from cave to cave in order to avoid too much contact with the outside world. Once, a group of hunters came into the area and mistook him at first for a demon or spirit. When they agreed to kill him, one of their number suddenly felt remorse and saved his life. Curious shepherds, and even robbers, made it necessary for Milarepa to keep changing households, pushing his way into even more isolated territory. To his sister Peta, who again sought him out, begging him to return to the world as a rich and comfortable self-respecting lama, he says:

Worldly acquisitions of wealth and the need of clinging to them, as well as the pursuit of the Eight Worldly Aims [comfort, misery, wealth, poverty, fame, obscurity, praise, blame] I regard with as much loathing and disgust as a man who is suffering from biliousness regards the sight of rich food. . . . Moreover, my guru, Marpa the Translator, bade me give up all worldly concerns, aims, and objects; bear the loss of food, clothing, and name; live in various solitary places . . . and carry on my devotions most energetically, giving up all prospects in this life. Such being my guru's commandments, I am fulfilling them.

Soon even his wretched aunt appeared at Milarepa's cave in hope of forgiveness and a blessing. Bound as a devotee of the Buddha to compassion for all beings, Milarepa took her in and preached to her several sermons on the laws of karma. The aunt was converted, did penance, and meditated, until even she achieved liberation.

Milarepa was ready to gather around himself a group of disciples in continuing the Kargyupta line bequeathed to him by Marpa. Among the people who gathered around him, twenty-five were saints. The rest were all enlightened to different degrees, according to their efforts and development. Many were women, many householders, and several important lamas themselves joined the band of Milarepa's followers. One such lama, Tsaphuwa, was a rich hypocrite, however. Outwardly, he pretended to love the master, but inwardly he spent his days hating and envying him. At last, unable to control his hatred after being humiliated by Milarepa at a public banquet, Tsaphuwa determined to kill him. Promising one of his concubines a precious turquoise jewel, he instructed her to feed Milarepa a dish of poisoned curds. The woman followed his instructions, but she became so frightened when Milarepa guessed her purpose—and ate the curds anyway—that she confessed and repented on the spot. But Milarepa had already determined that it was time for him to leave this world.

At a last gathering among his disciples, he sang them a group of hymns he had written. (Milarepa's hundred thousand religious songs are still in circulation.) The result was extraordinary. Highly developed disciples attained nirvanic consciousness; moderately developed students reached heights of supersensuous bliss and ecstasy they hadn't experienced before; and all others were immediately converted to the path of renunciation. Then he exhorted all followers—be they gods or spirits or men—to continue seeking even further states of religious communion. Informing them that he was about to leave this life, he instructed them to preserve his sermons and hymns, to make them part of everyday life. "If ye do this," he said, "in whatever realm I may arrive at the Perfection of Buddhahood, ye shall be the first body of disciples to receive the Truth that I shall then preach. Therefore rejoice in this."

Shortly after this assembly, he took ill and refused all medicines or expiatory rituals. "So be it."

> *All worldly pursuits have but the unavoidable and inevitable end, which is sorrow: acquisitions end in dispersion; buildings, in destruction; meetings, in separation; births, in death. Knowing this, one should, from the very first, renounce acquisition and heaping-up, and building, and meeting; and, faithful to the commands of an eminent guru, set about realizing the Truth [which has no birth or death]. That alone is the best ritual . . .*

Lama Tsaphuwa, the perpetrator of Milarepa's illness, came to see how the yogi was faring. Curious about the master's powers, he begged to have him transfer some of the pain to him, actually as a test, for he didn't believe in Milarepa's powers at all. Suddenly, as Milarepa (who was unwilling to make even Tsaphuwa suffer) sent the pain traveling across the room at the door, there was a loud splitting sound. Tumbling down in a heap of splinters, the door had assumed the force of Milarepa's agony; but Tsaphuwa would not rest until he himself had seen what the pain was like. Milarepa then transferred half of what he was feeling into the assassin's body. The lama nearly died on the spot. Then, overwhelmed with true remorse for the heinous crime he had committed, Tsaphuwa put his head beneath Milarepa's feet and confessed. Instead of admonishing him for his sins, Milarepa said: "May all thy evil karma born thereof be partaken of by me and thoroughly digested." Like a true saint, he had assumed even the terrible fate of his murderer. Tsaphuwa was so ashamed that he offered all his worldly goods to the master. But Milarepa had him divert them to the disciples instead. They, in turn, used them to defray the costs of Milarepa's burial, and later paid for religious observances. Tsaphuwa, now a convert, became one of Milarepa's true devotees.

Deciding to die in Chubar, quite a few miles distant, Milarepa—against the protests of his followers, who believed him to be too ill—"traveled" in many different bodily forms. Some of his disciples went on ahead and found that he had already passed them. Others followed later and swore that they attended him; still another group claimed to have seen him at the Poison-to-Touch Rock miles away. And yet, the one Milarepa was supposedly being escorted by a group of devotees on his trip to Chubar, while another preached a final sermon to a gathering at the Red Rock. His great spiritual powers had made it possible for him to appear to all of them. When asked about the phenomenon by the entire group who had come to Chubar, he said: "All of you are right. It was I who was playing with you."

Milarepa remained at the cave of Brilche in Chubar, where ecstatic visions and rainbows, and brilliantly illuminated mountain tops became the order of the day for all witnesses.

At last he called his people together and dispensed with his meager worldly goods: bowl, spoon, cotton cloth, staff—giving them as talismans and exhorting his disciples to renounce the world's vanities for the sake of Truth. Then, at the age of eighty-four, he sank into the final samadhi and died. It was the year A.D. 1135. All who were present suddenly observed marvelous phenomena. The sky was filled with colored designs, lotuses, and mandalas. The clouds were painted in wondrous colors and assumed the form of umbrellas, banners, draperies and ritual objects. Flowers poured down instead of rain; mountain peaks seemed to bow toward Chubar, and heavenly musical hymns of praise to Milarepa were heard. Many saw angels bearing gifts; the most advanced of them were enabled to converse with gods. For a few brief moments man was transported back to the Golden Age, and heavenly wonders were revealed on earth.

Someone tried to light the funeral pyre but was unsuccessful. Something was wrong—a favorite disciple was missing. This the closest students learned when they gathered around the corpse of the master, which had reanimated itself to explain. Rechung, the disciple who was miles away, had a vision of Milarepa beckoning him to come quickly to Chubar. With foreboding, he hurried to the place to find his guru's body on the funeral pyre, the crowd of devotees waiting, wondering what to do.

As soon as Rechung came near, the flames lit of themselves. Then, from the midst of the funeral fire, the form of Milarepa, with the right hand pressing down the flames, and the left hand pressed against his cheek, addressed them all, singing his final hymn. It is in this pose, and it is this scene that Tibetan artists have portrayed in religious paintings of Milarepa.

When the fire had died and the ashes were meted out to different followers, a strange will was found. In the paper,

Milarepa had written directions leading the disciples to a certain rock where they would supposedly find "gold." When they got there and uncovered the area, they found a square of cotton cloth covering a knife and a lump of brown sugar. With this, there was a manuscript.

> The cloth and the sugar, if cut with this knife, will never become exhausted. Cut as many strips from the cloth and bits from the sugar as possible and distribute them among the people. All who taste of this sugar and touch this cloth will be saved from the lower states of existence. These were the food and clothing of Milarepa when he was in Samadhi, and have been blessed by all previous Buddhas and Saints. Any sentient being who heareth the name Milarepa, even though it be but once, will not take rebirth in a lower state of existence during seven lifetimes, and for seven lifetimes will remember past lives. These things have been prophesied by the Saints and Buddhas of the past. Whoever shall say that Milarepa possessed hidden gold, let pollution be placed in his mouth.

Following instructions, the disciples cut the sugar into innumerable pieces; yet each piece was as big as the original, which itself was never exhausted. The cloth, too, was cut into innumerable squares, and, along with the sugar, was allotted to the people. Many who were diseased merely took a bite and were cured; others who were still bound to earthly desires turned to meditation at a mere touch of the cloth. And, say the witnesses, all retained their portions of sugar and cloth for as long as they lived.

(Overleaf) Here is Ramakrishna in an ecstatic state at the home of Keshab Sen, a famous intellectual reformer of India.

RAMAKRISHNA

In Kamarpukur, seventy miles from Calcutta, a boy named Gadadhar (Macebearer) was born to a poor Brahman family. It was on the eighteenth of February in 1836, and Khudiram, the father, was very careful in casting the child's horoscope because of a series of visions he had had pertaining to the birth. The family was already blessed with an unusual child, a boy named Ramkumar who had from early on displayed psychic abilities, and who was later to grow into a fine Sanskrit scholar as well. The odd thing about Gadadhar's birth—that is, besides the revelation of the god Rama as a boy to Khudiram in a dream—was that his mother Chandra was forty-five, and thought to be past her child-bearing years. Moreover, the couple were apart for some months, as the father had gone on a religious pilgrimage to another city, when each learned of Chandra's pregnancy. Khudiram returned after information from the god Vishnu (also in a dream) that he would be born to Chandra as a human boy. In the meantime, Chandra was experiencing visions daily as well, so that when the couple were reunited, each couldn't wait to tell the news they both had already gained on their own.

One day seven months later, Chandra left the child on the bed underneath the mosquito netting. Returning there, she saw an enormous man lying in the place of the baby, a stranger whose bulk filled the entire bed. She rushed outside in search of her husband, but when they came back together into the bedroom, Gadadhar lay on the bed under the mosquito netting as before.

The boy grew strong and healthy, and was very vibrant and loving, if a little on the stubborn side. At five, he started school; by the time he was six, he had undergone his first spiritual experience. Walking alone, he'd lost consciousness suddenly after having seen a dark raincloud and a flock of white cranes. It only lasted briefly, and when he got up he was perfectly well and happy. But fearing the effects of the evil eye or some other curse on the child, Khudiram removed his son from school.

In 1843, Khudiram died, leaving Ramkumar, the eldest son, as head of the household. Gadadhar grew more meditative and introspective after his father's death; he nestled closely into his mother more, and developed the habit of waiting on holy men who used to stop at a pilgrimage rest in town. His second spiritual experience came when he was accompanying a group of townswomen on a religious pilgrimage. As they were passing the statue of an Indian goddess who was to be the object of their worship, Gadadhar's body grew stiff and numb, tears flooded from his eyes, and everyone around him thought he had died. Crying out to the goddess by addressing the boy, the women were successful in drawing him back into consciousness. Again, as he had been the first

Kamarpukur, where Ramakrishna was born.

time, he was cheerful and showed no ill effects from his experience.

Another time, when playing the role of Siva (the god of renunciation) in a town pageant, he went into a trance state; this time, smiling, with tears rolling down his face, he stood onstage transfixed. The townspeople removed him, trying to revive him as they brought him home. Some thought he might be epileptic; others said he was crazy. This time Gadadhar remained in the trance for three whole days.

Ramkumar's psychic abilities unfortunately worked always on morbid events to come. Thus, it was with great sadness that he predicted his own wife's death in childbirth. The little girl that came from this sad event left him distant and cool, so that soon after he could easily leave her with his mother and make for Calcutta, where he opened a Sanskrit school.

Gadadhar got along extremely well with his little niece, and it was with great disappointment that he left home on Ramkumar's orders to assist him in his Calcutta teaching venture. Though sixteen, Gadadhar still lived the life of a naïve and cheerful little boy in many ways. School never agreed with him; for three years Ramkumar tried to convince him to become a serious student—without success. Instead, he helped earn a living for the family by performing Brahmanic priestly functions in the homes of wealthy people, who, incidentally, found him as charming and likable as did the villagers back home.

When Ramkumar became the Brahman priest for a Kali temple in Calcutta, Gadadhar went with him. As assistant priest (accompanied by a younger nephew named Hriday) Gadadhar assumed the name Ramakrishna. It was his job to dress and prepare the images in the temple for worship, and he took his job very seriously, as we shall soon see.

Ramkumar died in 1856; Ramakrishna was now twenty years old. A vast change overcame his personality, for he spent every waking moment seeking for a vision of Kali. This period marks his entry into what Indians call sadhana, religious preparation for enlightenment, which often entails much psychological and spiritual suffering. Ramakrishna's vision of Kali did not come before he had shed many tears and lived through many bizarre and ascetic sufferings.

There was an unbearable pain in my heart, because I couldn't get a vision of Mother [Kali]. Just as a man wrings out a towel with all his strength to get water out of it, so I felt as if my heart and mind were being wrung out. I began to think I should never see Mother. I was dying of despair. In my agony, I said to myself: "What's the use of living this life?" Suddenly my eyes fell on the sword that hangs in the temple. I decided to end my life with it, then and there. Like a madman, I ran to it and seized it. And then—I had a marvelous vision of the Mother, and fell down unconscious. . . . It was as if houses, doors, temples and everything else vanished altogether; as if there was nothing anywhere! And what I saw was an infinite shoreless sea of light; a sea that was consciousness. However far and in whatever direction I looked, I saw shining waves, one after another, coming towards me. They were raging and storming upon me with speed. Very soon they were upon me; they made me sink down into unknown depths. I panted and struggled and lost consciousness.

A street scene in Kamarpukur.

From that point on, Kali appeared to Ramakrishna almost continuously in his mystical visions. To calm down his ecstatic state, his mother had him return to Kamarpukur. Hoping that the local exorcist would relieve her son of his "abnormal" state of mind, she convinced him to remain at home for a while. It was then 1858, the middle of his most intense period of sadhana. The exorcist, of course, proved unsuccessful, relieving the young man only of a bad habit he had of chewing on betel nuts, something like chewing on tobacco.

Still Ramakrishna continued haunting burial grounds and other lonely places, meditating on Kali, whose favorite locations are those connected with death. Undaunted, Chandra persisted in her efforts to "normalize" her son. What better than to provide him with a wife! When they could find no family willing to put up a daughter for the odd young man with visions, Ramakrishna himself informed them of the divine choice of bride he'd already seen in his meditations. Saradmani, daughter of Ram Mukjopadhyaya, lived in another village; she was then five years old and the bridegroom twenty-three, but the match was made.

Unlike other typical Hindu husbands of the period, Ramakrishna allowed the girl to live with her parents until she had come of age. Then, instead of treating her in the usual way, that is, making a servant of her, and a kind of legal concubine without rights, Ramakrishna educated Saradmani, looking after her as a father would, and serving her in many ways as if she were an embodiment of the goddess Kali herself. While the little girl remained back home, he again returned to the temple and found himself now completely overcome by mystical states.

No sooner had I passed through one spiritual crisis than another took its place. It was like being in the midst of a whirlwind—even my sacred thread was blown away . . . sometimes I'd open my mouth, and it would be as if my pains reached from heaven to the underworld. "Mother!" I'd cry desperately. I felt I had to pull her in, as a fisherman pulls in fish with his dragnet. A prostitute walking the street would appear to me to be Sita, going to meet her victorious husband [Rama]. An English boy standing cross-legged against a tree reminded me of the boy Krishna, and I lost consciousness. Sometimes I would share my food with a dog. My hair became matted. Birds would perch on my head and peck at the grains of rice which had lodged there during the worship. Snakes would crawl over my motionless body.

Things grew so bad that he stopped sleeping for six years. His eyes remained wide open and he lost entirely the power to blink his lids. Tears followed ecstatic visions and vice versa. The body lost all importance and, as in the case of all the other mystics we have discussed, there was no longer any emphasis whatever placed on physical life. Doctors could not help. Only one of them saw that Ramakrishna was suffering from spiritual, not physical, suffering during all those years.

Then one day as he sat on the banks of the Ganges, a woman in her late thirties appeared in a boat, making her way toward him. When she alighted, she announced that she was a member of a sect that worshiped the *Shakti*, or female aspect of God. The Bhairavi, as she was called, said that she had come at the urge of divine inspiration to seek him out and worship the god that resided within him. Every day after that, they sat and talked, she playing the role of both teacher and devotee. The burning sensations that Ramakrishna had been experiencing in his body vanished after she interpreted their cause correctly and then treated him. The Bhairavi claimed that she had read of similar symptoms in the case of the saint Sri Chaitanya, also believed to be a reincarnation of Krishna, also born on February eighteenth. To relieve Ramakrishna of the affliction, she chose the appropriate scriptural remedy, placing a wreath of fragrant flowers around his neck and anointing his body with sandalwood paste.

Seeing that all her predictions and analyses of this "avatar" had proven correct, the Bhairavi then challenged two of the greatest religious scholars in the area to debate on the subject. One arrived, took one look, and immediately agreed with her. There was no doubt that Ramakrishna was an incarnation of God; no *human* could sustain such ecstatic states for so long without dying. The other pandit, who possessed psychic intuition, also immediately agreed. There was no debate on the subject.

Many monks and laymen came to worship him, but it was not to be until fifteen years later that he would gather his true disciples. Ramakrishna waited patiently, for he had learned early of his long wait in a vision. In 1863, perhaps at peace with the unusual situation by now, his mother came to live at the Kali temple near him. With the "Bhairavi Period" now on the wane, Ramakrishna turned next to a wandering ascetic for lessons in an entirely new form of worship. Naked, tall, and severe, Tota Puri arrived at the Kali temple and, immediately approaching Ramakrishna, selecting him from a group, said: "You look as if you were fit to practice the Vedantic sadhana" (the most intellectual, nondualistic philosophy of the Vedas,

This is the place in Dakshineswar where Ramakrishna was sitting on the day the Bhairavi approached him in her boat.

the earliest Hindu scriptures). Ramakrishna went into the temple and asked for Kali's permission to enter Tota Puri's worship "without form."

After only a few months under the tutelage of the Vendantist holy man, Ramakrishna achieved the highest form of samadhi (transcendent bliss), that which goes beyond even images of deity, beyond all ideas of self and non-self, beyond all concept of duality. He became truly at-one with God.

No type of religious experience was closed to him after that. Ramakrishna, hungry for *all* forms of religious bliss, practiced even Moslem and Christian rites—much to the shock and displeasure of the orthodox Hindu establishment. He was mad, they said. Some could excuse him on these grounds, others could only wonder what he was up to. Nevertheless, to prove the unity of all faiths, he worshiped God in the form of Allah and Christ as well.

The Reality is one and the same; the difference is in name and form. There are three or four ghats on a lake. The Hindus, who drink water at one place call it "Jal." The Muslims at another place call it "Pani." And the English at a third place call it "water." All three denote one and the same thing, the difference being in name only. In the same way, some address the Reality as "Allah," some as "God," some as "Brahman," some as "Kali," and others by such names as "Rama," "Jesus," "Durga," "Hari."

Meanwhile, he continued behaving in his own unique, and often incomprehensible, way in the company of his patrons. Mathur, the wealthy benefactor of the Kali temple, saw almost immediately that Ramakrishna was a true holy man. He therefore devoted himself entirely to serving the eccentric Brahman priest, even to the point of distributing money to the poor at Ramakrishna's demand. The ecstatic trances came so frequently that it was hard to keep up with him; Mathur had to resort to providing him with a cart and having him wheeled around so that he wouldn't fall down and hurt himself when entranced.

Even Hriday, Ramakrishna's skeptical nephew and attendant, began to believe in his saintliness. It happened this way. One night, seeing his uncle walking toward the meditation grove that had been prepared for Ramakrishna a short distance away from his quarters, Hriday followed him with the intention of bringing his towel and water bowl. As he followed behind Ramakrishna, he suddenly saw his uncle's body grow full of light as it walked. No human being strode before him, but a transparent body of light, which now illuminated the entire meditation grove, lighting up trees, ground, and sky.

The figure of Ramakrishna, he saw as he looked on, was not walking but seemed to be floating a few inches above the earth. Hriday tried shaking himself out of what he thought might be an hallucination. But no matter how much he rubbed his eyes and pinched himself, he continued to see the vision. Suddenly he looked down at himself and realized that he, too, was shining and luminescent, that he had "caught" some of the afterglow of Ramakrishna's own light. He cried out: "Oh, Ramakrishna, you and I are the same! We are no mortal beings! Why should we stay here? Come with me, let's go from land to land, setting men free from bondage!"

Ramakrishna turned and shushed him. Seeing the young man's excited state, he quickly put his hand to Hriday's chest and prayed for Kali to make him gross again. It happened too quickly for Hriday, and he began to weep. "Why did you do that to me, Uncle? You have taken that blissful vision away from me! Now I'll never have it again."

Ramakrishna comforted him, saying that he only wanted to quiet him down for fear of waking everyone in the temple compound. Then he added, "If you only knew how many visions I have, every day! And do I raise such a racket? You're not ready for visions yet. The time will come for them."

But the experience had only whetted Hriday's appetite for more. In secret, he headed for the same meditation grove on another night, this time sitting down on his uncle's very spot. But Ramakrishna too had decided to go out that night— luckily for the adventuresome Hriday. As soon as Ramakrishna got within a few feet of his accustomed seat, he could hear Hriday shouting for help.

"Uncle, save me! I'm being burned to death!"

But there was no fire, and Hriday looked perfectly intact. When Ramakrishna asked what was wrong, Hriday said: "No sooner had I sat down in that spot, than it was as if a plate of live charcoal had been thrown right over me!" Ramakrishna, admonishing his nephew, passed his hand before his body and the burning immediately stopped. Promising him that he would get all the "spirit" he needed by merely serving him, Ramakrishna this time succeeded in convincing Hriday to stay away from the meditation grove. He had been, literally, playing with fire that he was not developed enough to control. For many years Hriday served Ramakrishna, but he was often given to capricious outbursts and sometimes even cruel tricks. The extraordinary spirit of his saintly uncle could only rub off on him to a small degree; the rest was a product of Hriday's own unfinished earthly karma.

After many years of yearning for his own true disciples, Ramakrishna was rewarded at last. In 1879, two agnostic cousins who had been influenced by the praises of Ramakrishna given by Keshab Sen, a famous Indian intellectual and reform leader, came to see the phenomenon of Ramakrishna for themselves. Ram Chandra Datta was a doctor who, after himself receiving spiritual vision, became a devoted "householder disciple" of Ramakrishna. There were to be mainly two groups of constant devotees at Dakshineswar—site of the Kali temple—over the years. One consisted of the outer circle of worldly people who continued in their jobs and family life; the inner circle was composed of monks who had renounced the world entirely and given all of their faith to Ramakrishna. More of these later.

Manomohan, a businessman cousin of Ram Chandra, the doctor, also gave up his agnosticism and joined the first group of disciples. The interesting thing about these people is that many of them came reluctantly or out of curiosity at first. Hardly any were "religious" to begin with; many were intellectual rationalists who wished to disprove the Ramakrishna "phenomenon," but who stayed on as converts. Surendra Nath Mitra, a well-to-do young man who liked to drink and run after women, turned eagerly to Ramakrishna for guidance. He wanted desperately to be spiritual, but just could not give up his wine. Reading his thoughts (something Ramakrishna was to do repeatedly with the many people who came to see him from far and near), the saint said: "Don't give up the wine. Offer it first to Mother Kali and then drink it as her food offering. Only you must be careful not to get drunk. Don't let your footsteps stumble or your mind wander. At first, you'll feel only the kind of excitement you usually feel; but that will soon lead to spiritual joy."

Many worldly devotees followed soon after. Most of them remained, bringing gifts, problems to be solved, good wishes, and a desire for spiritual uplift. But even more important, Ramakrishna now began to see the beginnings of a movement around him.

Latu, the first of the monk disciples, was a poor servant of the doctor Ram Chandra Datta. A proud, plain-spoken young man, he had become so enamored of Ramakrishna after having accompanied his boss to the temple, that he asked Ram Chandra to let him become Ramakrishna's servant; and the doctor agreed. Latu was so devoted and earnest a disciple that when Ramakrishna rebuked him for sleeping in the evenings, he gave up sleep entirely in favor of nightly meditation. Throughout his life Latu remained illiterate, childlike, and thoroughly faithful. His form of worship and worldly renunciation was to serve Ramakrishna day and night.

Gopal Ghosh, an older man recently bereaved at the loss of his wife, came to Ramakrishna for consolation. Not only was the widower lifted out of his depression, but he remained at

Dakshineswar, becoming an indispensable administrator whom Ramakrishna used to jokingly call "the overseer" because he was so properly organized.

Rakhal Chandra Ghosh (no relation to the first) came, like Latu, when he was a boy in his teens. Raised in a wealthy landowner's family, he was called Rakhal in honor of the god Krishna's cowherder friends. At school in Calcutta, he had met a boy named Naren, and together, they were to be the leading disciples and founders of the Ramakrishna Mission.

Rakhal was a very special case. Ramakrishna had prayed for a long time, hoping that Kali would send him a loving disciple very much like himself. A few days after approaching the goddess, he saw in a vision a boy standing nearby under a tree. In another vision after that, Kali placed a young boy on his lap and said: "This is your son." On the day that Manomohan (Rakhal's brother-in-law) came accompanied by the boy, Ramakrishna saw a lotus on the Ganges and two boys dancing there. One of them was the god Krishna; the other was the human boy Rakhal.

Oddly enough, Rakhal arrived by boat that very day. But Ramakrishna didn't show any surprise; instead, he sat and talked with him as if they had been old friends. Soon Ramakrishna began to assume a whole new identity: he became Yashoda, the foster mother of Krishna, and so acted like Rakhal's mother. Even stranger than this was the fact that Rakhal—only a teen-ager then—was able to understand and respond to Ramakrishna appropriately. It was as though the two had recognized each other and merely picked up where they had left off in another lifetime. Rakhal was always to have a special place in Ramakrishna's heart, and he became the first president of the Ramakrishna Society after his beloved teacher died.

Narendranath Datta, Rakhal's Calcutta classmate, was a

wealthy boy who had grown up in a family headed by an atheist lawyer father, whose own father had given up the world and become a monk. Naren, born on January 12, 1863, was to become world-famous as Swami Vivekananda, a holy man—almost as though he had skipped back a generation over his father and imitated his saintly grandfather instead. Yet the lawyer's rationalism and intellectual hunger made its mark on the young man. Naren's friends remembered him always as being highly spiritual and highly temperamental, both. His gnawing intellectual doubt led him to question all and everything that came in his path. He met his greatest conflict and greatest glory when he was asked to sing at a friend's home— for Ramakrishna was one of the invited guests. Naren had a magnificent voice that moved the saint to tears. Yet, even though he doubted Ramakrishna's sanity at first, he could not avoid visiting him to test him over and over again never realizing, of course, that it was *he* who was being tested all that time.

Later, as Swami Vivekananda, he recalled a startling early encounter with his soon-to-be guru:

As soon as he saw me he called me joyfully to him and made me sit down on one end of the bed. He was in a strange mood. He muttered something to himself which I couldn't understand, looked hard at me, then rose and approached me. I thought we were about to have another crazy scene. Scarcely had that thought passed through my mind before he placed his right foot on my body. Immediately, I had a wonderful experience. My eyes were wide open, and I saw that everything in the room, including the walls themselves, was whirling rapidly around and receding, and at the same time, it

147

seemed to me that my consciousness of self, together with the entire universe, was about to vanish into a vast, all-devouring void. This destruction of my conscious self seemed to me to be the same thing as death. I felt that death was right before me, very close. Unable to control myself, I cried out loudly, "Ah, what are you doing to me? Don't you know I have my parents at home?" When the master heard this, he gave a loud laugh. Then, touching my chest with his hand, he said, "All right—let it stop now. It needn't be done all at once. It will happen in its own good time." To my amazement, this extraordinary vision of mine vanished as suddenly as it had come. I returned to my normal state and saw things inside and outside the room standing stationary, as before. . . .

On another such occasion, Ramakrishna learned who Naren "really was"—that is, which saint he had been in another incarnation. During this vision, Ramakrishna foresaw how and when Naren would choose to leave the world (a highly developed yogi often determines the time of his own death). Like Rakhal, Naren, Ramakrishna knew, was one of his "eternal companions," destined to form part of his circle for many centuries. But at the outset it was not all that easy. Naren, unlike the mild and willing Rakhal, was a skeptical intellectual who would take his time in joining the fold.

Ramakrishna eventually gathered sixteen monk disciples around him; six of them, he claimed, were "avatars"—divine incarnations of saintly beings who were reborn in human bodies in order to help mankind. This group included: Naren, Rakhal, Baburam, Niranjan, Jogindra, and Purna. Gopal Ghosh, the eldest among them, was the only man who had lived in the world as a householder; the rest were celibate monks who had pledged their lives to Ramakrishna when still young.

Among the worldly devotees was one Girish Chandra Ghosh (again, no relation to the other Ghosh), sometimes called the Shakespeare of the Indian stage. This brilliant and versatile writer, director, and actor was a drunkard and reckless bohemian who nevertheless found himself longing for realization of God. Strangely enough, he became one of Ramakrishna's most devoted and spiritual followers, so that even today there is a picture of Ramakrishna in most Calcutta theaters. Actors cutomarily bow to the image of the saint to commemorate his approval of Girish's art. As in the case of Surendra Nath Mitra, the first "drunkard-devotee," Ramakrishna did not reprove Girish for his life style, but told him to devote even his failings as an offering to God instead. In this way, he could point even the lowest element in a man upward. "It is in the nature of a child to soil itself with dirt and mud, but the mother does not allow it to remain dirty always. She washes it from time to time. Similarly, it is in the nature of man to commit sin; but if man is sure to commit sin, doubly sure is [it] that the Lord devises methods for his redemption."

In April 1885, Ramakrishna fell ill. At first it seemed he was suffering from a sore throat, that his exertions, public appearances, and ecstatic states had weakened his body to the point of physical breakdown. But it did not take long before the fatal nature of the disease was diagnosed by a sympathetic doctor, who, in the course of treating Ramakrishna, came to believe in his highly developed spiritual nature. Nothing could be done. Ramakrishna himself had a vision in which Kali had displayed to him many sores on his back, especially at the back of the neck and at the throat. It was, she indicated, as a result of all the evil karma he had taken on for the many people who had come to him merely to touch him and sit in his presence. Ramakrishna was resigned to his death.

On the afternoon of January 1, 1886, he seemed to be feeling better, and asked the doctors to let him take a walk in the garden of the house his disciples had provided for him. It was a holiday, and all the householder disciples were gathered there to attend the master in his illness. When he came down, there were at least thirty people gathered in knots in and around the house. Some of them followed him outside to a spot under a tree where he had stopped to talk with Girish Ghosh, the theater director.

"Well, Girish," he said, "I hear you're saying all these things about me to everyone, wherever you go. What is it you see in me, that you can say such things?"

Girish bowed before Ramakrishna and replied, weeping, "Who am *I* to speak of him? The sages Vyasa and Valmiki could have found no words to measure his glory!"

Ramakrishna beamed and addressed the entire gathering of disciples: "What more need I tell you? Be illumined!" As soon as he had fallen into ecstatic trance after uttering those words, the entire company felt itself overwhelmed with emotion. Gathering around him, they touched him and bowed, placing their heads on his feet in the customary disciple-to-guru salute. Crying "*jai* [hail] *to Ramakrishna!*" and accepting his touch, each went into a different form of samadhi. The degree of enlightenment depended on the moral and spiritual capacity of the student; some achieved supreme vision, while others were instantly enabled to undertake serious meditation for the first time in their lives. All agreed, however, that Ramakrishna had that afternoon erased any doubts they might ever have entertained about his divinity.

On August 16, 1886, early on a Monday morning, Ramakrishna went into *mahasamadhi,* the ultimate form of ecstatic bliss from which one does not return. He had determined the moment of his own death, but not before handing the gauntlet to Vivekananda, once the reluctant Naren and now his dearest disciple. The years after his death were to see even greater expansion of Ramakrishna's reputation. Vivekananda, blessed not only with spiritual vision but with worldly sophistication, intellect, and personality as well, put into action all of the saint's visions. With the financial backing of the householder and businessmen devotees, he established a mission, called The Ramakrishna Order, which built hospitals, schools, colleges, libraries, publishing houses, and clinics. The monks of this order work in these service centers part of the time and retreat for meditation the rest of the year. Devotees function in some charitable capacity or other in societies all over the world. There are over one hundred Ramakrishna Missions in India and Asia, ten in the United States, one in England, one in France, and one in Argentina.

Though he remained relatively unlettered throughout his life, Ramakrishna's spiritual message has touched the four corners of the earth.

BIBLIOGRAPHY

A. C. Bhaktivedanta. *The Teachings of Lord Chaitanya.* Bhaktivedanta Book Trust, 1968.

W. Y. Evans-Wentz. *Tibet's Great Yogi Milarepa.* London: Oxford U. Press, 1958.

Hakuin. *Selected Writings.* Tr. Philip B. Yampolsky. New York: Columbia U. Press, 1971.

Christopher Isherwood. *Ramakrishna and His Disciples.* New York: Simon and Schuster, 1970.

Thomas Merton. *The Way of Chuang Tzu.* New York: New Directions, 1965.

PERLE EPSTEIN is the author of *The Private Labyrinth of Malcolm Lowry*. Her three previous books for young people include: *Individuals All, The Way of Witches*, and *Monsters: Their Histories, Homes, and Habits*.